HERMAN MELVILLE

CW00969667

The
MANIFESTO
of
HERMAN MELVILLE

BARRY SANDERS

O/R

OR Books
New York · London

© 2025 Barry Sanders

Published by OR Books, New York and London

Visit our website at www.orbooks.com

All rights information: rights@orbooks.com

All rights reserved. No part of this book may be reproduced or transmitted in any form or by any means, electronic or mechanical, including photocopy, recording, or any information storage retrieval system, without permission in writing from the publisher, except brief passages for review purposes.

First printing 2025

Library of Congress Cataloging-in-Publication Data: A catalog record for this book is available from the Library of Congress.

British Library Cataloging in Publication Data: A catalog record for this book is available from the British Library.

The manufacturer's authorised representative in the EU for product safety is Authorised Rep Compliance Ltd, 71 Lower Baggot Street, Dublin D02 P593 Ireland (www.arccompliance.com)

Typeset by Lapiz Digital. Printed by BookMobile, USA, and CPI, UK.

paperback ISBN 978-1-68219-399-0 • ebook ISBN 978-1-68219-412-6

For Robert Falk, dear friend, who got this ship sailing.

In the Beginning, the Leviathan. In the End, the Cetacean. In between, Herman Melville's *Moby Dick,* difficult and dense, mythic, demanding intense concentration, the author's angry voice pitched high enough for the gods to hear. As contemporary reviews made clear, the work was convoluted, confusing, crowded with far too many words. People picked it up, determined to make it to the end, but many quickly surrendered.

Moby Dick is a story about a madman seeking revenge against a whale that "reaped away" his leg. To call that tale a cliché is akin to calling *Adventures of Huckleberry Finn,* a tale of two pals on a lazy float down the Mississippi, or Faulkner's "The Bear," a story about a boy's first hunt in the woods of Yoknapatawpha County. Such a reading of *Moby Dick* suggests that Ahab is entitled to seek revenge, the whale deserving of capital punishment.

Melville's career as an author is as odd as his work, which had its beginning, not behind a desk, but on the high seas. On January 3, 1840, having just turned twenty, he signed on as a "green hand" aboard a whaler named the Acushnet. Sailing out of New Bedford, the whaling capital of the world, the ship headed for the South Seas, then to the Marquesas Islands. An inquisitive, likeable and loquacious cabin boy, the captain, Valentine Pease, quickly promoted him to lethal harpooner.

That new assignment, which required of him to plunge harpoon after harpoon into the flesh of other sentient beings, quickly became more repulsive than the young Herman Melville could ever have imagined. And so, after two unbearable years of killing creatures on the high seas, he and his buddy, Toby, jumped ship in Nuku Hiva Bay, in the Marquesas, hiding out until a passing whaler, the Lucy, retrieved them. Several months later, this time in Hawaii, they jumped ship again. Having had his fill of adventure, and far too much of whaling and killing, Melville returned to Troy, New York, in 1844, to settle down and write. As he put it, later, to Nathaniel Hawthorne, "From my twenty-fifth year, I date my life." Over the next thirty or so years, until roughly 1876, Herman Melville came potently alive as enraged guardian of the natural world.

Melville wrote furiously, publishing two travel narratives: *Typee: A Peep at Polynesian Life*, in 1846, and in the following year, *Omoo: A Narrative of Adventures in the South Seas*. Works both highly metaphysical and spiritual followed in rapid order: *Mardi and a Voyage Thither* (March 16, 1849), *Redburn* (July 29, 1849), and *White Jacket* (February 1, 1850), all of which met with poor sales. In 1851, Melville marked the completion of his mighty *Moby Dick* by moving his family—his wife and two children—from New York to the heart of the Berkshires, to Pittsfield, Massachusetts, near his friend, Hawthorne, to whom he boasted: "I have written a wicked book, and feel spotless as the lamb." A few months later, in yet one more note about his dangerous creation,

2

Melville described the work of his lifetime, *Moby Dick,* as a book that had been "broiled in hell-fire."

In this country, no publisher was eager to publish a book with its prose on fire—impossible language and a tough moral stance do not make for big sales. Melville turned to England for help. After much wrangling, on October 18,1851, the London firm of Richard Bentley agreed to publish a modest 500 copies of Melville's sixth book, released in three volumes, titled *The Whale*, featuring, on its deep-blue covers, a group of small and sluggish Right whales. One month and far too many editorial changes later, the leading publisher in America, Harper and Brothers, on November 14, 1851, published in one volume, *Moby Dick; or, The Whale,* in a run of 915 copies, at $1.50—on its cover, the correct Sperm whale. Melville was pleased.

The feeling did not last long. Critics gave it tepid reviews, and sales were dismal. In both England and the U.S., *Moby Dick* was a resounding disappointment. Perhaps the theme of malevolent slaughter and destruction was not appealing in an era of American literature that confronted the most controversial social and political issues of the time. Literary historians have since crowned that phenomenal outpouring of literature, from the 1830s to the end of the Civil War, as the American Renaissance, the awakening of a cadre of literary giants in this country: Emerson, Hawthorne, Thoreau, Whitman,

Dickinson, and most ironically and terribly belatedly, Herman Melville.

A long tale inflected by religion, rage, and the condemnation of killing for profit was tossed aside by the critics as odd, obtuse, and, worst of all, irrelevant. As if a hunt for an albino whale was not strange enough, Melville gave readers a distended story about a sea captain, Ahab, and his deranged drive for revenge against— of all things—a huge fish. Reading his bloated descriptions, one might even accuse Melville, himself, of being slightly deranged: "All that most maddens and torments; all that stirs up the lees of things; all truth with malice in it; all that cracks the sinews and cakes the brain; all the subtle demonisms of life and thought; all evil, to crazy Ahab, were visibly personified, and made practically assailable in Moby Dick." How could Melville so ignorantly, or so willfully, miss the temper of the times? Or, more accurately, how could the critics so blatantly read past Melville's deeper meaning?

Most critics dismissed *Moby Dick* as derivative, shunting Melville aside as a mere hack, who had reworked an exhausted story about a Sperm whale named Mocha Dick that some thirty years earlier, on November 20, 1820, smashed the whaleship Essex to bits, killing every person aboard. Critics needed help, for more was at stake than a single whale and a ship. Armed with rage, Melville attacked the brute power, not of whales, but of those whom he knew could not turn aside from their commitment to destroy the entirety of the natural world. It was easy to miss the heart of *Moby Dick,* for nature writing in the nineteenth century favored the pacific and the Edenic, with reveries like *Walden,* or the surgically precise poems of Emily Dickinson, or the whimsical and thus only slightly frightening legends of Washington Irving. No one stood on a mountain peak to let fly an impassioned plea for justice, and certainly no one, in the newly-founded Republic, demanded such an outrageous move.

Melville moved beyond expectations, situating his veneration of the natural world in the ocean, where, in the ancient world, a congeries of more than fifty Greek gods and goddesses infused the beginning of life with spirit and magic, making the sea reverberate with the deepest and most surprising meaning. Drawing on an early definition of voyage, meaning "narration," Melville wrote his warning about the imminent demise of the created world, so shocking then, but close to cliche now—a world wickedly picked-apart, exhausted, poisoned, and tossed aside in shame and near total collapse. Melville made it plain that greed and arrogance would eventuate only in catastrophe. He called people to action, in part by writing beyond the familiar, in both theme and form. Herman Melville had delivered his manifesto.

Named for the Pequot Indians, who were wiped out in an act of genocide by a band of colonists, Ahab's whaling vessel, the Pequod, rides the waves as a ship condemned. Leaving port on Christmas day, Ahab opted for killing, revenge, and profit over celebrating the arrival of Christ. In time, Ahab will discover that which he hunts and hounds will turn against him; that it will reduce the Pequod to nothing but splintered wood and nails; and of the crew only one will manage to survive. That person, who has learned his lesson well—and it will not be Ahab—will deliver his own protracted warning to whoever will be willing to hear or overhear. We do not need to be told or scolded, but we ought to pay attention and listen.

For Melville's manifesto rested on the elemental, which sent him not just back to the ocean as the source of life, but to the ancient waters of Oceanica, back to Homer and to the *Iliad*, in which poem—and this must have appealed mightily to Melville—the first word out of the poet's mouth is *menin*, or "rage." Peter Sloterdijk, a contemporary German philosopher, wrote a startling book about that convergence of ocean and anger, titled *Rage and Time: A Psychopolitical Investigation*." In it, Sloderdijk underscores the fact that literature in the West gets launched in an anger that propels the action well beyond the usual expressions of that emotion: "At the beginning of the first sentence of the European tradition, in the first line of the *Iliad*, the word 'rage' appears. It appears totally and solemnly, like a plea, a plea that does not call for any disagreement." Its Latin root, *rabiens,* modern rabies, helps to explain outrageous, irrational

6

human behavior when it comes so closely to resemble the unpredictable behavior of a wild animal.

As a gift from the gods, Achilles must become infused with divine rage in order to free the City of Troy. Although an obvious and basic emotion, the word *rage* does not enter the English language, oddly enough, until the beginning of the fourteenth century, and then gets defined in extremes, either as mild "infuriation" or utter "madness."

In *Moby Dick,* Melville uses the word *rage* ten times, *outrage* once, *outrageous* three times, *madness* seventeen times, and *mad* a mighty thirty-six times. Ahab, in his diabolical manner, corrupts any vestige of the emotion's elevated, classical heritage. His leg gone, he rules with a blinding, uncontrollable, angry behavior that he passes on, like some rabid animal, his venom infecting the entire crew, transforming them from greenhands into delirious madmen, who come to hate life with all the intensity of Ahab's ragged heart.

Melville reinterpreted classical variations on rage, moving them beyond Ahab's in-grown rage, into the outrage that he wanted every reader to feel about the desecration of nature, beginning with the first harpoon that Queequeg threw with great might, piercing the flesh of his first whale. Melville knew that, left unchecked, the lustful pursuit of profit would have to destroy everything, starting with wonder and ending with the Earth itself.

To counter such a nightmare, Melville amplified rage into the more formidable outrage—inciting people, hopefully, to act. Only such extremes could conjure the responsibility needed to repair America's sense of morals and ethics and set the natural world back in order. Melville had been reading Homer, prompting him to situate his own adventure, not merely on the sea, but in the myth-drenched *Oceanica*, in which the first and mighty creatures mentioned in Genesis swim and play and feel so marvelously at home. Melville's own rage was ignited by the wholesale slaughtering of those Ur-creatures, those myth-makers, the mighty *Livyathans*. The slaughtering of those majestic beings is integral to the wicked calculus of capital, in which more killing means more profit. Melville focused on a single whale: To kill that wonder, named Moby Dick, was to extinguish for all time the embodiment of both magnificence and surprise. It meant the death of the sacred and the holy. It meant the end of a time.

In the middle of the nineteenth century, in order to defend the natural world, Melville abandoned the certainties and satisfactions of the novel for the unknown perils of something close to the ancient odyssey, making readers rethink the very idea of literature, itself—its assumptions as well as its usual emotional charge. Invoking Homer, Melville whisked readers away to another time, taking them on a distended odyssey, this time under the command of a madman armed with a corrupted agenda.

Whaling occupied a particularly distorted place in nineteenth-century commerce. Young whale killers were praised and characterized as warriors, who risked their lives on the stormy seas, to bring home much-needed oil so people could light their houses, prepare their meals, and read scripture far into the night. Such a gloss was easy, for the gore and the killing took place thousands of miles out at sea, out of view.

Melville knew the truth firsthand and up close, and he pressed it into people's faces. *Moby Dick* indicts the killing of the wonders that are whales, creatures that are emblematic of surprise and sheer astonishment throughout all of nature. Melville venerated those over-sized beings with an intensity so powerful that the theologian, Jacques Maritain, might have called it a "eucharistic passion in the heart of life."

Melville decided to tell his story from as close to a surreal but tragic and precarious perspective as possible, through a narrator, Ishmael, the sole survivor of the ship, alone and adrift in the vastness of a vast ocean, clinging to a coffin that had been built for someone else, but which now serves as his life preserver: Death and Life merge in a single piece of wood.

"Call me Ishmael," announces, or commands, the talking head. And thus, the extended tale begins. In the *Iliad*, Homer calls on the Muse, perhaps Calliope, to sing her song through the poet. Ishmael calls on the reader so that he begin his telling. We might be flattered, but for the moment, embued with the insight of Adam, we agree to name Ishmael, revealing his essence and identifying him as the figure on whom we depend for the telling of this most extended story. He will remain afloat so long as we keep listening. Melville has hooked us. Why did we agree to give him a name? Why did we not put the book down and silence this poor wretch? The answer reveals an underlying strategy in *Moby Dick*: To effect change, one must first assume responsibility, if not for the devastation, then for the care and recovery of the Earth.

Besides connecting with an odd narrator, we are also asked not simply to read, but to work our way through prose thick as blubber, to embrace sentences that crest and crash like huge waves: Line after line, the narrative changes but rolls on, for more than 800 pages and 134 chapters. For Melville will never let up, Ahab will never give up. Ishmael will never tire and give out. And that most formidable creature, Moby Dick, will never give in and go away.

And the reader? Well, like Ishmael, the reader feels more than a bit overwhelmed, ready to surrender, let go, and perhaps, at some moment, even to go under. What trap has Melville set here? Any trace of a plot seems to have migrated beyond the grasp of the reader, who is eager, even desperate, to make sense of so much pain and death, of so much killing and gore. Just as the story hits smooth sailing, Ahab erupts with a rant about whales or spouts some arcane passage from the Bible. Ishmael's own situation is revealed only a bit before the story ends. Readers might believe that Melville failed them on many levels or, even worse, deliberately ignored their expectations, but nothing is normal here—not subject, character, conflict, pace, or form.

Like Ishmael, Melville the author, and Melville the naturalist persisted. Even after *Moby Dick*'s dismal reception, Melville continued to write. He was but thirty-two years old when he published two more novels: *Pierre; or, The Ambiguities,* in 1852—which critics dismissed as "Herman Melville crazy"—followed by *The Confidence Man: His Masquerade*, published on April Fool's Day, 1857—which the critics, once again, panned as frivolous, and so much beside the point. It was his tenth work over only thirteen years, when even the seemingly indomitable Herman Melville, by all appearances, had had enough.

Weary of soul, his health failing, drinking more and more, Melville sorely needed renewal. On October 11, 1856, he left home for a personal hajj to the Holy Land, returning seven months later, on May 20, 1857. To earn some money, he tried the lecture circuit, but critics disliked his tentative style, and so, after three years, he seemed to give up totally. Disappointed and dejected, he left Pittsfield in October 1863 with his family—his wife, Lizzie, and four children—for Manhattan, to a house he had bought from his brother.

Three years later, out of a not-so quiet desperation, he settled for a job as a customs inspector and, for six days a week, checked the manifests of whaling ships against their inventory of carcasses, bones, and oil—an auditor of death—on the very docks where he had once denounced such killing. Melville passed his remaining nineteen years tallying the number of whales killed and the profits earned. After writing one of America's earliest and most assertive manifestos, Melville ended up certifying manifests.

By 1887, *Moby Dick* had passed out of print, having sold, over its nearly forty years, a spare 3,180 copies, a paltry eighty copies a year. In 1890, the New York *Times* printed an anti-obituary: "There are more people to-day who believe Herman Melville dead than there are those who know he is living. And yet if one chose to walk along East Eighteenth Street, New-York City, any morning about 9 o'clock, he would see the famous writer of sea stories—stories which have never been equaled."

Less than one year later, no one would see Herman Melville walking anywhere, for on September 29, 1891, the "famous writer of sea stories" died of "cardiac dilation." In his obituary, the New York *Times* praised *Mobie Dick,* describing Herman Melville, variously, as "one of the founders of Navesink, New Jersey," "a civil engineer," and one of "the best criminal lawyers in Connecticut." Even worse, the *Times* had printed Herman Melville as Hiram Melville.

Beyond the misguided reviews of his work, and the gauche declarations of his passing, the reality is that

Herman Melville died feeling that his call to action, *Moby Dick*, was a commercial and intellectual flop. The New York *Times* did not review *Moby Dick* until more than seventy years after its publication, on August 10, 1924, and then only because Random House had published, in sixteen volumes, *The Complete Works of Herman Melville*.

Something dramatic occurred to alter the reputation of that most massive, poetically conceived mammal and to hoist its author from substandard hack to utter genius. Even in these Tik-Tok inflected times, high school students, who may not have read a single word of the book, know that *Moby Dick* is a classic of American literature, and that at some time in their lives, they must read it—not listen to it as an audiobook—without understanding why.

Reading *Moby Dick* has become a rite of passage, a necessary part of a person's literate upbringing, a basic in America's real or imagined cultural cache, an essential work in any canon. Whatever this designation might mean—and it should mean a great deal—*Moby Dick* is decidedly, magisterially American. We may be cautious in reading it, because it is painful to understand the way it reflects the history of this country.

Why did it take seventy years after the book's publication, and one hundred years after the author's death, that is, not until the first decades of the twentieth century, and primarily through the insistence of a few key New

York academics, for critics to acknowledge *Moby Dick,* with its opening sentence having achieved near universal recognition, as a work of genius? The turnaround began nearly seventy years following the publication of *Moby Dick*, close to the centenary of Melville's birth, around 1919. It took a good deal of time for critics to understand his work. It took much longer for them to praise it. Such is the problem with the avant-garde.

After languishing for seventy years, Herman Melville, like his surreal surrogate, Ishmael, was snatched from going under, brought back onto dry land, and re-introduced to readers in what has been called, most generously, as "The Melville Revival." Considering its urgent message, delivered in such zealous language, it is not so surprising that, in the throes of an insistent, industrialized economy, along with a radical shift in aesthetics in which artists dispensed with subject matter, and writers disposed with plot, logic, and traditional word order, *Moby Dick* might be reconsidered experimental, avant garde, and even radical—a work in search of a genre. It took even longer for people to accept his screed against the killing of nature as a manifesto.

Critics began praising the book with sometimes-embarrassing, puffed-up superlatives—from the powerful to the prescient, from the experimental to the avant-garde—but arriving, generally, at a single declaration: *Moby Dick* had appeared well before its time. For those critics who penetrated its deeper meaning and its wider significance, *Moby Dick* came to life as a misunderstood masterpiece of American literature and longing, and got resurrected as one of this country's earliest examples of experimental, deeply political works of prose—a few critics even referred to it with that most elusive cliché: "The Great American Novel."

For far too long, readers ignored the book's prescience about the drive in America for unbounded wealth, most viciously realized in the destructive and lethal search for oil. But, finally, critics agreed: *Moby Dick* had been misread, misunderstood, dismissed, and thus it was forgotten. So dazzled, or confused were they by Melville's prose, few paid attention to his condemnation of America's greed and destruction.

In this country, the machine came to dominate everyday life much earlier and more powerfully than anywhere else, the "modern torment" becoming near intolerable, the tempo of life shifting abruptly and dissecting time more sharply. By the 1920s, the loud growl of horsepower had become deafening, drowning out any cries for logic and restraint, while the dislocations of daily rhythm insulted the usual and the expected. In a period punctuated by disharmony and piano compositions liberated by the improvisations of jazz, people began strolling to the downbeat of disregard—the age of swag revealed in the tempo of the swagger. In such a reordering of rhythms, Melville's "prophetic song" began to be heard more clearly and understood more definitively. Strangely, for people to slow down enough to care required something like a national nonchalance.

The dislocation of human sense ratios opened new possibilities for understanding *Moby Dick*, how it should be heard, and thus how Melville should be understood. Melville benefited from the disruptions in rhythm, reinforced by the pace and pitch of the new machines, the tempo of the expected and the regular getting out of the way to make room for the odd and off-beat. Ahab himself, a man "dismasted," one leg intact and the other fashioned from whale bone, moved across the deck of the Pequod off-beat and out-of-step.

After so many years, Melville's a-rhythms, or anti-rhythms, began to make sense, which meant that *Moby Dick* could finally be read, not just as a telling in a register unheard, but as a warning in a world dominated more and more by the obscene power and persistence of machines tearing up the land in search of gold, diamonds, and, of course, oil. Its meaning was more deeply revealed within its own rhythms and pace, within a prose seemingly at rest but where, aboard ship, words became so tempest-tossed they must be shouted into the wind to be heard, let alone understood. Certain it is that the wind will revolt, and that words and ideas, like startled gulls, will scatter this way and that. It took persistence and more than just a bit of desire, perhaps, but Melville began to be heard.

That strange, misunderstood book slowly made more and more sense in a world that had not just lost its sensibility, but a shocking number of its most noble creatures, whales, along with so many other worldly wonders—a decimation without protest, for the killing took place out of sight and without oversight, any right-thinking opposition occluded by the thrill of a bustling economy. As everything submitted to the will of the new entrepreneurs, the threat of disaster turned into a necessary tragedy, the price, as the saying goes, for doing business.

Herman Melville is one of those rare artists, possessed by the power, like a Hebrew prophet, to peer into the present and extract its meaning. He stood firm against the idea of killing nature so that entrepreneurs could make a killing in the marketplace. From his time aboard a whaler, he knew the grotesqueries of that killing, initiated by rage and finished off with harpoons, lances, and razor-sharp knives.

Moby Dick made most sense when placed within its proper genre. Melville had given his readers a huge book, with a title that explained little and a text that valorized a sea-born mammal of gargantuan proportions. Departing from any ordinary reading experience, he gave readers something so radically new, so dense and thick that, if they hoped to understand his creation, they would have to struggle with language, dig for meaning, and persist in their reading to the end. Signing on to such a voyage demanded work, hunting down and seizing the truth, as the story loomed through the fog of dense prose. Melville translated the wonder that once inhered in nature, when language invoked myth and magic, and naming creatures revealed their true essence.

Moby Dick reveals itself as a profound work, especially—I am tempted to say *only*—when it is placed in a more political, much more aggressive category than the novel, for Melville's subject simply offends: the ruthless assault on the natural world by human beings for profit. *Moby Dick*; or, *The Whale* is about gruesome, bloody acts of killing in pursuit of profit. Here was a warning, not presented as a Jeremiad—not as a scream or a screed, for such genres demand far too much cajoling—but, drawing on earlier forms to reveal the crisis of the moment, Melville seized on the manifesto.

Melville uses the word *manifesto* only once in *Moby Dick*, in an unsettling chapter, "The *Jeroboam's* Story." There, we learn that a whaling ship, the Jeroboam, named for the biblical king of Israel and which name translates in Hebrew to "pleading the people's cause," sails under the command of a Captain Mayhew. We also learn that the entire crew has been infected with a "malignant epidemic." Mayhew sights the Pequod and, knowing that his crew might infect others, decides to approach the Pequod alone in a small boat.

The Jeroboam has on board a greenhand, who the rest of the crew considers strange, but because of his "atmosphere of sacredness," also believe that he holds the power to foretell the future. His strange behavior, oddly, is reflected in his outfit: "A long-skirted, cabalistically cut coat of a faded walnut tinge enveloped him; the overlapping sleeves of which were rolled up on his wrists. A deep, settled, fanatic delirium was in his eyes." Stubb recognizes him as a well-known "scaramouch," a scoundrel from town, but who, aboard the Jeroboam, has "gained a wonderful ascendancy over almost everybody." The crew believes he can cast spells, and that he probably caused the epidemic.

That odd creature, whose oversized garment resembles the loose flesh of a whale, calls himself Gabriel, after the archangel celebrated for announcing the birth of Jesus, and who, now at sea, and in the tangle of death, predicts that he who tries to kill the white whale, will most assuredly die. That strange person more than predicts. Rather, as Melville writes, using the Homeric term for the ocean, Gabriel "published his manifesto, whereby he set himself forth as the deliverer of the isles of the sea and vicar-general of all Oceanica."

Ignoring Gabriel's warnings, Ahab asks Mayhew: "Hast thou seen the White Whale?" Before he can respond, Gabriel interrupts, once more, with his awful prediction. Elevating Moby Dick to "no less a being than the Shaker God incarnated," Gabriel warns Ahab to back off, for killing Moby Dick will result in a sin of the highest order and the greatest magnitude. Mayhew tells Ahab that the Jeroboam had, indeed, hunted down the Mighty White Magnificence, but when the first mate tried to drive a harpoon into its side, Moby Dick grew enraged, turning on its attacker, and crushing him to death. Mayhew has seen enough, and coupled with Gabriel's warning, has abandoned the hunt.

Gabriel escalates, ordering Ahab to stop his madness immediately. In the assuredness that characterizes a manifesto, Gabriel predicts that, like the first mate aboard the Jeroboam, if Ahab persists, he will perish. More than that, Gabriel foresees the death of every crew member aboard the Pequod, as well as the sinking of the ship itself. Allow the Holy Whale to live out its days. Let it swim in peace. Gabriel's words hang in the air, the crew silent and uncertain.

Melville knew whaling first-hand and up close, for at twenty-two years of age, as we saw, he had been immersed in the art of serial killing, the method of taking lives for profit. Melville's rage-infused Manifesto was informed by whaling as a model for the terror and torment that he predicted would be unleashed in the coming years, not just at sea, but across the entire country. Oversized, awe-inspiring, whales live not merely in the middle of the ocean, but many fathoms below the surface, out of our line of sight but not beyond our imagination. No incantation, and certainly no machine, however powerful, can rouse them from their underwater dreams. They move at their own pace and respond to their own needs. They sidle effortlessly into our own dreams and fantasies—emblems of the unbelievable—nudging aside the hugest of creatures. Periodically, they must break the surface for a draft of air and reveal themselves to us as living testimonials to all that we thought unbelievable.

Melville installed the whale as nature itself. He took readers on their personalized, protracted voyage of destruction and killing, to a reality far beyond any literary genre, to a declaration, personal and pointed, about the inevitable degradation of the natural world by the greed of deeply committed, disoriented entrepreneurs. Generating enormous profits through killing—with Ahab as CEO of Death—whaling provided the model of brutalizing capitalism that has helped bring us to our environmental catastrophe. People who lit their oil lamps, cooked their food, concocted their margarine, lubricated their machines, wore perfume, or forced their way into corsets, unwittingly supported the grotesquerie of death on the high seas. The price of luxury was catastrophically, even unknowingly high. In the late Forties, most surprisingly, sperm oil was even needed for fabricating the uranium-fueled atomic bomb.

It was the 1850s, a period of radical mechanization and thus a period, as Melville saw it, ill- suited for relaxed reading, in which in the rich loam of ease, indulgence, and languor, the horror of injustive thrived. Melville demanded analytical thinking, pondering, and action, repulsing his readers with descriptions of the natural world hacked to bits and sold off in the marketplace.

This massive book—and, for its very subject, it must be massive—is Melville's alarum, his scream in the face of humanity's fast-approaching midnight, a catastrophe concocted in the middle of the ocean, with far too much gall, gore, and disregard of life, and with far too much devotion to profit. *Moby Dick* warns of an insanity that, in a capital economy, promotes the rampant slaughter of its most majestic creatures.

The period saw an explosion in the number and might of machines, many of them designed to dismantle the natural world in what has been most generously crowned, the Industrial Revolution. Melville knew what havoc those machines would eventually create. With a demand for a more plentiful and cheaper oil to keep the new machines firing, entrepreneurs turned to the land and to its hidden wealth. Whaling had inscribed the way to wealth: Destruction without penalty, killing without consequence, wealth without guilt, the disappearance of the natural world without a whimper from anyone.

By forcing oil to the surface, slowly at first, and then more rapidly and violently, early prospectors methodically and, without pausing, poisoned the planet. The natural world traded places with the Leviathan, dismantled for its treasure, bit by bit, until the Earth, itself, earned its place on the endangered species list. *Moby Dick* marks a decisive break with the world of letters, demanding to be read as both scream and screed, as a withering of traditional forms, situating itself as a warning about a catastrophe unthinkable and oh so chilling—the end of all life.

For Melville, such horror began with killing those sanctified creatures from Genesis, whose magnificence, under the aegis of commerce, were reduced to a natural resource. If we will it, whales must surrender their lives to the higher demands of luxury. Against relentless progress, the majestic and the marvelous must perish. To succeed, commerce must dispense with sorrow, regret, or even discomfort. The only noun that matters is the common noun, profit, for without more and more of it, capitalism sputters and dies, and so the devastation must increase in number and in scope. Ahab knows he is right to feel as he does, for that dumb creature, the whale, refuses to submit to his will. After all, he has named the whale and so he must own it. It disobeys him and so it must die.

Melville decries those who hold in their hands the lives of sentient creatures. Aboard a whaler, life turns grotesque, an insult to the idea of being civilized. Killing hundreds of thousands of whales out of view insulated the industry from criticism. Besides, people needed oil, soap, perfume, umbrellas, and fishing rods. When the lust for oil moved on land, in plain view, the demand for other essentials blinded people, once again, to the killing. Besides, federal laws protected corporations from being sued for their havoc, permitting them to assault the Earth so fundamentally they altered the very nature of weather patterns.

23

By the middle of the nineteenth century, people were more fascinated by the might of steam-powered machines than by the wonders of the natural world. Vision shifted and values changed; the tempo of life accelerated; the natural world overtaken by the dynamism of the dynamo. Power revved up its nasty rule. In 1830, the first steam-powered locomotive reached a top speed of fifteen miles per hour. A mere ten years later, in 1840, in a land grab of monstrous proportions, this country boasted 3,000 miles of track, on which trains chuffed along at sixty miles per hour.

Manufacturers introduced those new machines as outlandishly powerful and utterly essential, causing them to proliferate rapidly, threatening to take over the real world and to take charge. On May 1, 1851, only five months before the publication of *Moby Dick,* that futuristic, machinic world premiered at the Crystal Palace, in Hyde Park, England. Known as the Great Exhibition of the Works of Industry of All Nations, it was organized, in part, by Prince Albert, husband of Queen Victoria, who sanctified the 14,000 machines on display as "the greatest achievements of science and technology toward the realization of the unity of mankind." To walk inside the Crystal Palace was to peer into the next century, one dominated by the hydraulic press, the vertical printing machine, the image telegraph, the repeating handgun and rifle, and the flush toilet.

At the center of the Exhibit stood the behemoth of a steam engine, invented by an American, George Henry Corliss, which rose over forty feet, and weighed an astonishing fifty tons. For the Exhibit's grand opening, President Grant flipped a switch, setting into motion the machine's unbelievable 1,400-horsepower, allowing it to run day and night until the Exhibit closed, on October 15. How could any literary or artistic creation—anything, indeed, from the artist's imagination—ever hope to outshine the high-speed whine of such a gargantuan dynamo? More than one newspaper article concluded that even though it had opened in England, the Great Exhibition provided a glimpse of "American power and technology."

In its first six months, an astonishing, unbelievable six million people visited the Crystal Palace. After more than a five-month run, on October 15, the Great Exhibition closed, three days before Richard Bentley published *Moby Dick*—a literary work without machines, as the Pequod sailed with the wind, its captain navigating the enterprise by sighting celestial bodies, the crew killing the bounty of the sea by hand. While the Exhibition promoted surprise and astonishment, Melville favored its opposite, outrage, for he was far less concerned with what machines might create, and much more concerned with what they could destroy.

Melville left the land, in favor of a seemingly endless but classical voyage, sailing into a hallucinatory horizon, headed into a reality radically alien. Melville is attempting, most mightily, to make sense of what he felt aboard a whaling ship, and how the men around him coped with their destiny with death. Looking over a wide expanse of water to the far edge of the horizon, Ahab's crew attempted to make out, not only the largest animal in creation, but a true sport of nature, a bright white whale, the first "rapture of the deeps." But such a phenomenon is not so easy to spot, for along with fog and confusion, that madman, Ahab, demands that his crew see what he needs them to see, what he wants them to believe.

Among a mighty host of other things, *Moby Dick* is a voyage that forces the senses into high alert, for sailing in the ocean demands an acute sense of smelling, seeing, hearing, and an awareness of a tingling on the skin, an aesthetic awakening to a white dot in the middle of nowhere, knowing that bit of nothing as something huge, as *that* whale. The chance to destroy that miracle of nature does not become a possibility for readers until chapter 132—out of a total of 134—titled "The Chase—First Day." In the chapter, the possibility of killing brings the ship's captain, that is, Ahab, to a full and invigorating life.

On the evening before the eventual show-down with Moby Dick, Ahab "suddenly thrusts out a face fiercely, snuffing up the sea air as a sagacious ship's dog will, in drawing nigh to some barbarous isle. He declared that a whale must be near." Ahab smells oil at its base level, as the Latin verb *olere* means "to emit a smell." Those who detect its presence do so like animals after prey. Ahab sniffs out the truth, impressing the crew with his superior sense . . . of everything: "'What d'ya see? cried Ahab, flattening his face to the sky. 'Nothing, nothing sir!' was the sound hailing down in reply." Ahab knows better. He knows that the whale, that huge cache of oil, must be lurking close by. The men cannot see, and certainly cannot smell, and thus cannot know. But Ahab's senses have turned primal, made somewhat exquisite and supernatural by the intensity of his rage, by his hatred concentrated on that one creature. Rage sharpens the senses and hones animal instincts. Scent alerts us to the sacred. Perfume is made from ambergris, called "floating gold," removed from the Sperm whale, prompting Melville to describe a dead whale from which "stole a faint stream of perfume."

So that he might take in the entirety of the ocean, and to confirm the power of his senses, Ahab commanded the crew to hoist him to the top of the royal-mast head. From that perspective, like a living banner, he could lord it over those under his command, proving that he was truly gifted and, most importantly, utterly correct. Melville takes charge: "Two thirds of the way aloft, and while peering ahead through the horizontal vacancy between the main-top-sail and top-gallant-sail, he raised a gull-like cry in the air. 'There she blows—there she blows! A hump like a snow-hill! It's Moby Dick!'" Moby Dick is nature, itself, "a snow-hill." Ahab, too, merges with the natural world, uttering "a gull-like cry in the air." And so, while Moby Dick breaches, in need of air, Ahab descends the mast to rob the creature of its breath. The warning on board: "A dead whale or a stove boat!"

How to understand any killing, large or small, and certainly one aimed at the sacred whale? How to explain the swatting of a fly and the harpooning of the whale as something other than scale, meaning, or intention? Just exactly what is the relationship—one on display in Eden—between seeing and owning, seeing and disobeying, seeing and the ultimate—devouring and thus knowing? What, if anything, can one reasonably say about the killing of a magnificence like the whale, even when—or especially when—the killing purports to be carried out in order to satisfy people's needs, such as oil?

In a chapter titled "The Lamp," Melville rhapsodizes about the lust for whale oil, even aboard ship, boasting that "in merchantmen, oil for the sailor is more scarce than the milk of queens." Then, in Melville fashion, he goes further: "See with what entire freedom the whale man takes his handful of lamps—often but old bottles and vials, though—to the copper cooler at the try-works, and replenishes them there, as mugs of ale at a vat. He burns, too, the purest of oil, in its unmanufactured, and, therefore, unvitiated state; a fluid unknown to solar, lunar, or astral contrivances ashore. . . He goes and hunts for his oil, so as to be sure of its freshness and genuineness, even as the traveller on the prairie hunts up his own supper of game." Whale oil is as essential as food, the killing is incidental.

As a Manifesto mourning the eradication of wonder in the world, *Moby Dick* is a powerful indictment of this country's ruthless economy, a time when machines, in their inexhaustible power, began to assume a sublime status, the mechanical taking charge over the natural, the machine over the human. Melville warns of that rapidly approaching mechanized, brutalized, and racially charged world under the thumb of commerce, fueled by greed, and magnified by massive earth-devouring machines. He warns of the oncoming, mad control of the new legal outlaws, the Robber Barons, a term which first appears in 1859, to describe a band of well-dressed thieves, free of morals or ethics, and decidedly free of limits on their plundering.

Melville's Oceanica Odyssey was an indictment of exploitation and ruin—of plantation-owners, who increased profits by stealing entire families from Africa and bringing them to the American South, as enslaved machines; of ranchers who, empowered by the Indian Removal Act, seized land by marching people of the Cherokee Nation, some 16,000 men, women, and children, in 1838, 1,200 miles on the "trail of tears," forcing those who survived—a bare 12,000—onto reservations west of the Mississippi; and of moguls who, in 1860, conscripted peasants from China to complete the building of their transcontinental railroad.

In the name of progress, early colonial entrepreneurs deemed it essential, for some reason, to drive the passenger pigeon into extinction, to eradicate nearly all the bison, wolves, deer, and other creatures on the plains, to kill untold numbers of tribal peoples, enslaving millions in the budding democracy that seemed to require monumental acts of desecration, destruction, and eradication.

Mark Twain called the period from 1870 to the end of the century the Gilded Age, a time of gross materialism and political corruption, informed by the philosophy of the richest man in the world, Andrew Carnegie. Twain meant the term *gild* as a fake, a mere treatment of a surface, in imitation of the real thing, gold. Carnegie championed the new world in his essay, "The Gospel of Wealth." Competition, he preached, was "good for the race, for it makes for the survival of the fittest"—and by race, of course, he meant "the white race." The American Way guaranteed that "hard work and perseverance pay off."

Melville warned readers that those new, powerful machines, coupled with the drive for wealth, would lead to the destruction of the natural world. As a Manifesto, *Moby Dick* demanded that readers do more than just come awake, as earlier religious revivals had commanded. To save their home demanded the boldest action. In the most radical way, *Moby Dick* can be read as America's first call to action, alerting every citizen to a looming catastrophe. In the 1850s, such a warning would have sounded far-fetched and bizarre—how insane to speak of the finality of a living thing like nature, itself. We read *Moby Dick* with hindsight and wince.

To underscore the likelihood of such a catastrophe, we have the word of the narrator, who has survived the heart of darkness and has risked his life to tell the truth. He narrates, not as we have come to expect, as a character in control, but just the opposite. At any moment, Ishmael might run out of air, go limp, and disappear; but he continues, for he knows his tale is essential. He embodies the precarious. And so, we enter the story, our guide not so much a narrator as something closer to a powerful witness, an outsider who describes the nature of fallen human nature in a carefully metered sentence, one close to homily: "For there is no failing of the beast of the earth which is not infinitely outdone by the madness of man." Ishmael has witnessed such failing at its worst, such as the killing of the whale in Chapter 62, so innocently titled "The Dart," but which Ishmael calls "Murder," and which might be renamed as a massive bloodletting:

> From the vibrating line extending the entire length of the upper part of the boat, and from its now being more tight than a harpstring, you would have thought the craft had two keels—one cleaving the water, the other the air—as the boat churned on through both opposing elements at once. A continual cascade played at the bows; a ceaseless whirling eddy in her wake;

and, at the slightest motion from within, even but of a little finger, the vibrating, cracking craft canted over her spasmodic gunwale into the sea. Thus they rushed; each man with might and main clinging to his seat, to prevent being tossed to the foam; and the tall form of Tashtego at the steering oar crouching almost double, in order to bring down his centre of gravity. Whole Atlantics and Pacifics seemed passed as they shot on their way, till at length the whale somewhat slackened his flight.

"Haul in—haul in!" cried Stubb to the bowsman! and, facing round towards the whale, all hands began pulling the boat up to him, while yet the boat was being towed on. Soon ranging up by his flank, Stubb, firmly planting his knee in the clumsy cleat, darted dart after dart into the flying fish; at the word of command, the boat alternately sterning out of the way of the whale's horrible wallow, and then ranging up for another fling.

The red tide now poured from all sides of the monster like brooks down a hill. His tormented body rolled not in brine but in blood, which bubbled and seethed for furlongs behind in their wake. The slanting sun playing upon this crimson pond in the sea, sent back its reflection into every face, so that they all glowed to each other like red men. And all the while, jet after jet of white smoke was agonizingly shot from the spiracle of the whale, and vehement puff after puff from the mouth of the excited headsman; as at every dart, hauling in upon his crooked lance (by the line attached to it), Stubb straightened it again and again, by a few rapid blows against the gunwale, then again and again sent it into the whale.

"Pull up—pull up!" he now cried to the bowsman, as the waning whale relaxed in his wrath. "Pull up!—close to!" and the boat ranged along the fish's flank. When reaching far over the bow, Stubb slowly churned his long sharp lance into the fish, and kept it there, carefully churning and churning, as if cautiously seeking to feel after some gold watch that the whale might have swallowed, and which he was fearful of breaking ere he could hook it out. But that gold watch he sought was the innermost life of the fish. And now it is struck; for, starting from his trance into that unspeakable thing called his "flurry," the monster horribly wallowed in his blood, overwrapped himself in impenetrable, mad, boiling spray, so that the imperilled craft, instantly dropping astern, had much ado blindly to struggle out from that phrensied twilight into the clear air of the day.

And now abating in his flurry, the whale once more rolled out into view; surging from side to side; spasmodically dilating and contracting his spout-hole, with sharp, cracking, agonized respirations. At last, gush after gush of clotted red gore, as if it had been the purple lees of red wine, shot into the frighted air; and falling back again, ran dripping down his motionless flanks into the sea. His heart had burst!

"He's dead, Mr. Stubb," said Daggoo.

"Yes; both pipes smoked out!" and withdrawing his own from his mouth, Stubb scattered the dead ashes over the water; and, for a moment, stood thoughtfully eyeing the vast corpse he had made.

Melville moved American literature beyond fiction, past Emersonian self-reliance or Whitman's self-assurance— Melville much preferring self-assertion—in order to realize a looming catastrophe that few of his readers would have ever noticed: The killing of nature at a brisk pace. Once we allow the book to unfold as a dire warning, what we once believed shatters like the Pequod itself. Did we know that reality could be so easily dismantled; that creatures could so easily disappear and in such gross numbers; that commerce was so painful; and on and on? Should we have cared more than we did—paid more attention, taken immediate action? Could the splintering of the ship of state be the central image, the disaster to which we must all attend. Is Moby Dick the hero?

Only after the shipwreck do we realize that Ishmael has been narrating the entire story up to his neck in water. To hear Ishmael clearly, Melville also pitched his readers into the sea: A tale of the sea must be narrated in the water, a tale of the fragility of the natural world must, itself, be fragile. We know nothing about Ishmael's precarity until it is too late—leaving us afloat with an informant we have named and unwittingly saved. The reality surprises and shocks, realizing that we must be

34

close by to hear him out; that we must be in the sea, where both life and wholesale killing began.

Unable to tolerate that killing he knew much too well, Melville needed to write in the most dramatic way. He shipwrecked his readers, setting them adrift, unprepared and disoriented, in order to underscore the fragility of life, itself. To speak of dire consequence, as Melville must, is to risk sounding overwrought and out of touch—of being far too emotional. To say something honest and true, in the world of *Moby Dick*, is to sound deranged. The bearers of truth are not to be trusted. Soothsayers interrupt and they often disappoint.

Such is the cost, the attendant dangers, of speaking up and speaking out, of uttering the truth. A novel simply cannot manage Melville's outsized vision, Ahab's temperament, Moby Dick's majestic power, and Ishmael's fortitude. Melville needed to startle, upset, and perhaps above all, to shock—risking the reader's frustration. He found his footing in the manifesto. For the novel deliberates, cultivates whatever is reasonable, and reaches for clever conclusions. The novel often prompts a review and even a discussion of its ideas. But then the telling ends. The experience might linger, the images shimmering for a time but, again, the reader feels no call to action. For Melville, the novel had become a luxury.

One can pause in a work of fiction, back up, and reread some interesting or perplexing passage. Fiction promotes both forgetting and remembering, disengangement as something natural and without consequence. A reader can, of course, always put a book down or, as some of Melville's critics might have preferred, "throw it against a wall," hoping to crack its spine. The novel prompts a range of responses.

Not so the manifesto. With its argument and demands, the manifesto focuses. Relentless, even a bit reckless, the manifesto gets under the skin of anyone who dares read it, demanding they go on alert and, to repeat—for it cannot be said too often—to take decisive action. The manifesto also assaults, forcing readers to move beyond merely paying attention, beyond the cliché of taking some story to heart. It pushes people into the issues, roughs them up and puts them on the spot—forcing them to be decisive or to leave. It demands and compels. The manifesto puts up its metaphoric mitts, with bruising sentences intended to hit hard enough to leave a person unsettled, wondering what just happened. Relying on shock and outrage, the manifesto is a staging platform for taking bold and sometimes frightening action.

Manifestos rest on that one primal emotion, *rage*, encouraging people to refuse oppression, unwilling any longer to accept the accepted. Outrage might follow, a stab against the stubbornness of the universe, a stance that Melville found most dramatically expressed in Hawthorne. In a letter Melville wrote to his friend, dated April 1851, he practically anointed his pal: "There is the grand truth about Nathaniel Hawthorne. He says

No! in thunder; but the Devil himself cannot make him say *yes*. For all men who say *yes*, lie; and all men who say *no*—why, they are in the happy condition of judicious, unencumbered travellers in Europe; they cross the frontiers into Eternity with nothing but a carpet-bag—that is to say, the Ego."

Readers are not accustomed to a prose style, over such a protracted length, that resounds with the insistence of rage, threatening to devolve into outrage, driven to the extreme of Hawthorne's majestic *No.* To maintain its intensity for over eight-hundred pages, rage requires the lungs of Aeoleus. Readers tend to revolt, for the Manifesto places a burden on them, which Melville makes immediately apparent: "Call me Ishmael," someone says, setting the narration in motion, but it comes only after events have ended, and thus it becomes a retelling, a rebirthing. A biblical name provides this unknown with a much-needed history and personality. His opening sentence is not a command and not an ultimatum. No one, so close to drowning, would have the nerve to insist on such things. He merely needs a name. To be without one is so unthinkable that, in the Middle Ages, a person without a name is labelled *uncouth,* "unknown," not a part of the kith and kin, both cast-out and an out-cast.

In order to regain some identity, this sea-soaked unknown has relied on a religious figure who, like himself, is both orphan and exile, son of Abraham and the Egyptian slave Hagar. Such a battered, beleaguered, and misunderstood soul, such a so-called illegitimate offspring, this Ishmael will be the reader's guide in an extraordinarily long tale. And thus, our introduction to Ishmael, asking us, a stranger, to name him, and to reaffirm that he exists. And, if we agree, then we too sign on for a long voyage and a very long tale recounted by a character with a tremendous ability to remember, to understand and, most important of all, to change.

And so, by assenting, we climb aboard the Pequod, Ishmael recalling every detail for us—including the goriest acts of killing—taking the recollected voyage with him. We will participate, in a most vicarious but detailed way, in butchering the largest creatures in the world. Closing the book, we will wonder where we have been, what has happened, what we did, and why we delight in such exquisitely elevated prose about such a hideously degraded death. We will shake off the gore of adventure for the truth of our circumstance: Melville will have made us culpable.

And so, even if we stop reading and put the book down, Ishmael has assumed the power of his biblical incarnation, whose own skill at storytelling takes hold of us—although we know not his true identity, and although we might not accept the bible as the guide to righteous behavior. Those nineteenth-century readers who know their bible well will compare Ishmael with his namesake, his conversion measured by his salvation.

As Manifesto, *Moby Dick* is loaded with many tricks of persuasion and conviction, all of them intended to outstrip the strategies of the well-turned novel and subvert its usually comforting characters and reassuring tone and theme. After reading *Moby Dick*, no one says that was a most satisfying experience. A person is more likely to complain that such reading was grueling, arduous, painful, and often strangely mysterious. One feels virtuous in having finished it. Melville will have his way, for he is intent on making us react to those willful destroyers of nature, and determined to reveal, in the end, the precarity of the telling and the fragility of our own assumptions.

He also makes us see, and this is crucial, that the killing will not stop, for the new machine-driven, hellbent-for-profit world, by design, must expand and do so ever more powerfully. *Moby Dick* as Manifesto situates itself, again, in the sea where life, adventure, and narration all began, and to which Melville added a kind of ur-killing. Ishmael supplies the ardor that is rooted in biblical narrative. God-fearing, he has chosen an appropriate name, for in Hebrew Ishmael translates as "God Hears": All that Ishmael thinks, believes, and says, God overhears. Ishmael speaks, and we hear the truth. Curiously, throughout the entire trajectory of the narrative, we never see Ahab and Ishmael speaking to each other. Ahab knew to stay clear, for the madman fears that Ishmael will not only deliver the truth, he will also spread it around.

In the interval between silence and bombast, between rage and the truth, Ishmael has been able to hang on to his life. In asking to be named, Ishmael speaks with Adam's power, in which names of things reveal their essence, and thus Ishmael's self-selected identity. He asks to be named after the killing is over, for he has become critical of the enterprise of whaling. His name records his rebirth, announces his new identity and attitude. We must lend an ear so that his word will be heard, not by seabirds, or even by God, but by his kin. For language, too, having been corrupted, must be reconstituted, starting with the sole survivor, Ishmael, and shifting to the reader, as sole bystander. Ishmael calls on us, and in an odd way, also invokes us. We must respond.

In bearing at least an echo of God's Word, then, the Manifesto, even though it is coercive and intolerant of equivocation and defection, makes clear the insidious social and political conditions that constrain freedom and demand resolution. Manifestos insist in a way that even the most powerful novel could never tolerate, in part because—especially true of modern manifestos—they are written collectively, the passion of an individual moves into the compassion of co-conspirators. Melville forces the reader into conspiring, in the root sense of "breathing with" the narrator, a luxury since every breath may be his last. We begin this oversized tome, unwittingly, by colluding with the ideal, by taking on an enormous responsibility as something more than readers.

We no longer read as casual outsiders, then, or idle observers, but have been forced into sentences, syllable by syllable, as participants inside the events themselves, for we have named the narrator and we now hold a privileged relation with him and with language. As insiders, events slowly unfold and implicate, even suffocate, and by indirection, make us culpable in the action. We set sail with that madman of redemption, Herman Melville, and must say goodbye—to who we were and what we once knew—as well as to the solid footing of the land.

To close the book, to put an end to the narration mid-telling, would mean to drop our commitment to Ishmael, cutting our ties and letting him down, literally—for he will drown. As co-conspirator, the reader will bear responsibility for his death. In a flash, we realize that we have entered a trap, with his life now in our hands, with us responsible for keeping him alive, implicated in the plight of our fellow beings—both human and animal.

In the oddest, most convoluted way, Melville hands us the responsibility of bringing Ishmael to life and, through his wile, of keeping him alive. Indeed, responsibility is one of the keys to the meaning of *Moby Dick*. With the book's opening three words, a shrunken sentence with monumental implications, we begin reading with a responsibility for the narration and end by taking on the responsibility for the state of nature. The reader, as implicated or perhaps as a highjacked accomplice, is given a charge, a sense of urgency that says: to save the everyday, you must move into action. The Manifesto is intolerant of smiles of delight, or sighs of relief, or even easy nods of agreement. It assigns responsibility and then demands action. It irritates rather than satisfies.

Thus, the Manifesto holds readers hearts to their words and their feet to the fire. For those who craft any manifesto expect nothing less than a total defense of the truth in the public square, as the document makes its case, immediately, boldly, and relentlessly, locking in its argument and throwing away the key. The Manifesto demands a response beyond mere resistance. It aims for a change in people's perception and beliefs, and demands that they stop capitulating to a society that, in order to maximize profits and power, must control and destroy. The Manifesto has little patience for those who move through life half-awake, as somnambulists or zombies. In the end, one question matters—how committed are you to us and our mission? For Melville, that means one thing only: All killing must stop.

In this country, the spirit of the Manifesto has prompted a series of powerful, decisive statements and mass actions, in political struggles that, over time, erupted into a full and fiery life, most markedly in organizing committees, uprisings, strikes, protests, freedom marches, sit-ins, lie-ins, love-ins, anti-war actions, occupations, takeovers, and those early but most effective actions that hit at the heart of commerce and racism, like the Montgomery, Alabama bus boycotts, which began on December 1, 1955, when Rosa Parks was arrested for refusing to give up her seat to a white commuter in the front of the bus and take one in the back. Her refusal hit at the economy of Montgomery for a prolonged, painful 381 days. The loss of revenue forced the issue to the Supreme Court, which ruled, on November 13, 1956, that the segregation of public transportation violated the due process and the equal protection clauses of the fourteenth amendment to the Constitution. The boycott ended a month later, on December 20, 1956. Rosa Parks, the courageous activist, took great delight in her victory: "The Montgomery boycott became the model for human rights throughout the world." She had, indeed, become her own, living manifesto.

The country was founded, after all, on a manifesto, which opens with a shock: "When in the course of human events, it becomes necessary for one people to dissolve the political bonds which have connected them with another . . . " That same spirit informed Elizabeth Cody Stanton's Manifesto, at the Conference for Women's Rights, in 1848, in Seneca Falls, New York, which begins: "When in the course of human events, it becomes necessary for one portion of the family of man to assume among the people of the earth a position different from that which they have hitherto occupied . . . "

On July 5, 1852, Frederick Douglass, one of the first to sign the Manifesto for Women's Rights, standing behind the lectern in the Corinthian Hall, in Rochester, New

York, delivered his own Manifesto to the crowd, taking for his title the question: "What to the Slave is the Fourth of July?" Douglass' defiance, along with the sit-ins by four young black men, from North Carolina Agricultural and Technical college, at the F. W. Woolworth lunch counter marked for "whites only," in Greensboro, North Carolina, on February 1,1960, inspired a senior at Spelman College, Roslyn Pope, a founding member of the Atlanta Student Movement, and who, with Julian Bond, wrote, in March, 1960, "Manifesto: An Appeal for Human Rights." Two years later, some fifty politically enraged and deeply engaged college students, who called themselves Students for a Democratic Society (SDS), gathered in Port Huron, Michigan, from June 11 to 15, 1962, to expose the secret intent of American foreign policy. As if the idea and certainly the ideal of democracy had fallen ill and needed resuscitation, they drafted their *Manifesto to Revive Democracy*, an ideology that informed the New Left and helped inspire and later direct the Anti-War Movement, against Vietnam, beginning in the mid '60s.

The SDS Manifesto, essentially written by Tom and Casey Hayden, shouted to America: "We are people of this generation, bred in at least modest comfort, housed now in universities, looking uncomfortably to the world we inherit," and demanded the liberation of the United States' young people on the guiding principle of a totalizing "participatory democracy." The *Manifesto* relied on the philosophy of the Student Nonviolent Coordinating

44

Committee (SNCC), founded in 1960, and its demands for the equal rights of all people and the adoption of the tactics of non-violence.

In Oakland, California, two college students, Huey P. Newton and Bobby Seale, believed that such a commitment to non-violence doomed Black folks. And so, in October 1966, the two men frightened a great many white folks, and put every cop on alert, by founding the Black Panther Party for Self-Defense, making public its demands through conviction and alliteration: "All Power to the People. Black Power to Black People. Panther Power to the Vanguard." On May 15, 1967, the Panthers issued their Manifesto in what Newton and Seale called, The Ten-Point Platform and Program: "What We Want Now!"

Two years after the founding of the Black Panther Party for Social Justice, on June 28, 1969, and following a violent police assault on a gay bar—the Stonewall Inn, on Christopher Street, in Greenwich Village—gays, lesbians, and transvestites took to the streets, protesting wanton and arrogant police brutality. Those five days of struggle, known as the Stonewall Uprising, led to the formation of the AIDS Coalition to Unleash Power, or ACT UP, which, by 1987, became the Gay Liberation Movement. In 1990, ACT UP issued its *Queer Nation Manifesto: Urgent Political Power of Rage and Refusal.*

In a manifesto that does not get much attention, but which has assumed great historical significance, on July 9, 1955, some ten years after the bombing of Hiroshima and Nagasaki, Bertrand Russell and Albert Einstein made public their fear about the possibility of "universal death" in a document they drafted, which has been dubbed the Russell-Einstein Manifesto. Eleven other scientists signed, including Max Born, Linus Pauling, and Joseph Rotblat, who, in 1995, was awarded the Nobel Peace Prize. Einstein had died three months earlier, on April 18, making the Manifesto one of his last written statements, and his boldest warning about the end of humankind through nuclear madness.

In the face of such a horrendous possibility as the end of civilization, two of the most well-known, well-respected intellectuals in the world, a philosopher and a scientist, could reach the only sane conclusion: "In view of the fact that in any future world war nuclear weapons will certainly be employed, and that such weapons threaten the continued existence of mankind, we urge the governments of the world to realize, and to acknowledge publicly, that their purpose cannot be furthered by a world war, and we urge them, consequently, to find peaceful means for the settlement of all matters of dispute between them." Russell read the Manifesto aloud in a press conference in London, on July 9, prefacing the event in his usual understated way: "I am bringing the warning pronounced by the signatories to the notice of all the powerful Governments of the world in the earnest hope that they may agree to allow their citizens to survive."

In an almost parenthetical note, but one that follows on the common sense of Einstein and Russell and thus warrants more attention, Wendell Berry, this country's beloved political upstart as farmer, published, in 1973, his "Manifesto: The Mad Farmer's Liberation Front," which opens with an homage to the ironic: "Love the quick profit, the annual raise/Vacation with pay, want more/of everything ready-made. Be afraid/to know your neighbors and to die," and ends by swapping irony for honesty, anger for instruction, the overweening hubris of humans for the quiet instinct of animals: "Be like the fox/who makes more tracks than necessary, /Some in the wrong direction. /Practice resurrection."

By the end of the twentieth century, the manifesto, in its tone, language, and level of rage, all rise, close to the level that Melville had reached. The subject, amplified, remained the same—the destruction of nature, no longer by the ravages of some drilling or scraping machine, but through the impact of technology. In September, 1995, Theodore Kaczynski, who the press dubbed the Unabomber, mailed his ramped-up, 35,000-word indictment of contemporary life, which he titled *Industrial Society and Its Future,* to the editors of *The Washington Post.* If the editors were willing to publish it, Kaczynski promised to stop his campaign of terror. And publish it they did, the document became immediately and widely known as the Unabomber Manifesto. The search was on for this so-called madman.

Over the course of an incredible twenty years, Kaczynski was responsible for killing three people with mail bombs and injuring over twenty more. All of his victims were connected to technology in some way or other. While Kaczynski had gone somewhat mad, and for reasons radically different from Captain Ahab—in fact, for having to endure what an Ahab's madness had inflicted on the natural world—he had begun life as a brilliant scientist, enrolling in Harvard at sixteen and later teaching in the mathematics department at UC Berkeley. Considered a crazy killer by many, his manifesto is informed by the work of the great French technology theorist, Jacques Ellul, and the work of the early environmentalist, Rachel Carson.

Kaczynski blamed the degradation of daily life on what is now known as the technological revolution. Kaczynski's outrage erupted before the proliferation of laptops, the development of the World Wide Web, cell phones, podcasts, text messages, and social media platforms. Invigorated with the passion of a poet, of a revolutionary, he wrote a one-man manifesto, long and larded with facts, arguing that technology uproots the unpredictable pleasures of the wilderness, and ransacks humanity at the level of its very soul: "The Industrial Revolution and its consequences have been a disaster for the human race. The bad parts of technology cannot be separated from the good parts . . . We give up a piece of ourselves whenever we adjust to conform to society's standards.

That, and we're too plugged in. We're letting technology take over our lives, willingly." Such a surrender of power must stop!

In our own times, the unleashed, unbridled spirit of the manifesto continues that same kind of intense, angry expression, most notably in the popular outrage that followed on the killing of George Floyd by a police officer in Minnesota. The Black Lives Matter Movement promoted a Manifesto demanding that people say out loud the names of every Black man, woman, and child who had been killed, over the previous five or six years in this country, through the excessive force of the police. No mere exercise, it made people realize what it meant to have a name and to build a most complicated life inside a name, inside an identity. And thus, the plea, call me someone, and do it now! In some ways, we are all Ishmaels. Call our names out loud, and bring us back on board the ship.

Inspirited by one manifesto after another, political action has so deeply inflected the history of this country that it helped to carve the contours of its character: Truth must be exhumed and it must be sounded aloud, broadcast to those who still have the capability to hear. And so, strikes and demonstrations, sit-ins, and the occupations of buildings, offices, open spaces, and even that most sacred piece of turf known as Wall Street, leave their mark as advances toward the liberation of people in this, our political history.

In almost all of these remarkable instances and events, so-called minorities have provided the moral compass for the nation, pointing the direction in which we the people must move our hearts and heads, our feelings and our feet. We can, of course, give a name to that desire that so badly needs to be satisfied, to that goal that preempts all others: It can be nothing less than Liberation. For liberation is righteousness making good on its promise of equality.

Which could never be Melville's word, certainly, and definitely not his intent—the idea of righteousness—but it is an essential element, nonetheless, for nothing less than the survival of this planet. For the Earth must be liberated from the domination of capital exploitation and immense greed; it must be stopped from being destroyed by corporations insulated, completely, by the law from crimes and punishments. Such a break from madness will be difficult, but it is more than crucial. It is critical. For the Earth can no longer support our voracious, endless appetite for more and more fossil fuel. The ultimate manifesto might call for the liberation of the Earth from our own selves.

We must all realize now what once only the religious fringe and a band of survivalists believed: The End is nigh, and it is, indeed, the upending of the Earth—a horror that hundreds of scientists have confirmed, now, as inevitable unless we shut down the emission of all greenhouse gases—and even then, we may have passed the fail-safe moment. Those biblical predictions of the world being consumed in the brimfire of justice, in the flood-waters of mercy, have become grim and secular certainties.

The calculation is beyond imagining, for we face the collapse of the entire planet, the probability of the end of all life, both civilized and wild. On August 9, 2021, the UN released its Sixth IPCC Assessment on Climate Change, which its Secretary General, Antonio Guterres, called "a Code Red for Humanity." He delivered the news stripped of embellishment: "The alarm bells are deafening, and the evidence irrefutable. Greenhouse gas emissions from fossil fuel burning and deforestation are choking our planet and putting billions of people at immediate risk." The 2022 Assessment issued more of the same warning, for once again, to no one's surprise, there had been no change and thus no improvement and, alas, no hope.

To put an end to such a deranged drive toward our own self-extinction demands action beyond anything any of us has yet imagined, an extraordinary, revolutionary shift in thinking about our place in, and our connection with, the entirety of creation. The prospect of the end of life on Earth should shock each one of us into becoming a fully alive, living manifesto, dedicated solely, entirely, and most powerfully to preventing the wholesale extinction of all life.

Melville hated his time aboard a whaler. Back home, he thought deeply, became enraged, and began to write. On August 4, 1847, Melville married Elizabeth Shaw, the daughter of Lemuel and Elizabeth, the two families having shared a long and intimate history. After his own father died, young Herman relied on Lemuel for both succor and counsel. So close were they that one year before his marriage, in 1846, Melville published *Typee,* which he dedicated "To Lemuel Shaw, Chief Justice of the Commonwealth of Massachusetts, This Little Work is Affectionately Inscribed by the Author." Over the years, his relationship with his father-in-law shifted dramatically, grew more and more difficult and even fraught, their political views about human life and dignity diverging radically.

As Chief Justice, Shaw was responsible for generating a great deal of the outrage against the destruction of nature and that his son-in-law, Herman Melville, came to indict. For Shaw was not just any Chief Justice and his court no ordinary assembly. Monumentally conservative, Shaw presided for three decades, from 1830 to 1860, as the most powerful Chief Justice of the most influential court in the country, the Massachusetts Supreme Judicial Court. Through the exercise of his judicial power, Shaw ensured the rapid decimation of America's waterways and open spaces. Over his career, he adjudicated 2,200 cases, the overwhelming number of them resulting in laws that accelerated the expansion of the railroads, that increased the public utilities, and most pointedly, accelerated the unbridled exploration of oil and minerals across the country. Shaw wrote the controversial law enabling the "taking" of land through "eminent domain," which encouraged railroads to expand by seizing public land for its right-of-ways, and oil companies to drill deeper and more widely by taking Indian territory. More than that, he made mining and fossil fuel companies immune from all lawsuits—from the killing of people to the massacre of nature.

Chief Justice Lemuel Shaw passed more legislation than any other single figure in the history of the United States. Because of him, massive oil spills in the oceans that have killed unimaginable numbers of animals and wiped out miles and miles of plant life, get reconfigured, under his many layers of law, as mere accidents. Such missteps may prove lethal for the environment, but the law, nonetheless, regards oil spills, no matter the size, as a risk of doing business. The poisoning of aquifers must also be understood as necessary, which means that people can expect to contract various cancers from drinking tap water. Shaw guaranteed that no corporation, and certainly no officer of any corporation, could be held responsible for . . . well, anything. Shrug off the killing and destruction, for there are continents to conquer, and a world-wide economic power to launch. There are fortunes to be made.

In order for Americans to attain maximum wealth, Lemuel Shaw argued, the country must run its businesses with the cheapest labor possible, which meant enslaving Africans. To make certain that those people would not contaminate the purity of the white and the elect, Shaw became the author, in 1850—one year before the publication of *Moby Dick*—of the insidious "separate but equal" doctrine, writing that "racial prejudice is not created by law, and probably cannot be changed by law." The Supreme Court did not overturn Shaw's Doctrine of Separate but Equal, so named to gloss over its racism, until 1954, with its landmark ruling in the case of Brown versus the Board of Education.

There is a hint of redemption in *Moby Dick*, a glimmer of the humane. For such is the intent of the Manifesto, the promise of natality, the hope of beginning again and anew. The sea is the beginning of life, the whale the first sentient creatures named in the Bible. Melville lets us know that Moby Dick, a Sperm whale, has sexual affinities with its name. Ships, remember, remained at sea without returning home for four or five years. Melville describes the passion, perverted as it was, generated by those unhouseled men, over time, through killing their kin—mammals. The most potent of which—the Sperm whale—the crew celebrated in their daily ritual of pressing lumps out of its oil.

Such ardor particularly infected Ishmael, who refers to the use of sperm oil as a "favorite cosmetic," imbued with transforming power: "Such a clearer! such a sweetener! such a softener! After having my hands in it for only a few minutes, my fingers felt like eels, and began, as it were to serpentine and spiralise." Ishmael loses himself, his fingers lengthening into serpents, moving in spirals—leviathan-like—while caressing that miraculous essence.

After a few minutes of squeezing the oil, the usually becalmed narrator turns rhapsodic, visionary. "Squeeze! squeeze! squeeze," he shouts, surprised by the level of his own passion: "All the morning long; I squeezed that sperm till I myself almost melted into it; I squeezed that sperm till a strange sort of insanity came over me; and I found myself unwittingly squeezing my co-labourers' hands in it, mistaking their hands for the gentle globules."

The sudden touch of flesh makes him aware, not just of the absence of real human contact aboard ship, but of the inhumanity that pervades nearly everything they do. Unabashedly, he seizes the moment to announce the importance of his mistake, combining images of male with female, as he pleads with his crewmembers to melt into each other: "Oh! My dear fellow-beings, why should we longer cherish any social acerbities, or know the slightest ill-humour or envy! Come; let us squeeze hands all round; nay, let us all squeeze ourselves into each other; let us squeeze ourselves universally into the milk and sperm of kindness." Ishmael raises high his plea for friendship, a manifesto, of sorts, for renewal and natality. With kindness in short supply, he calls them home as "dear fellow-beings." Over the course of the story, it is Ishmael who comes to see the horror in whaling, the tragedy in the killing of those monumental creatures of the sea.

While Melville may be giving us a glimpse of the power of the ecstatic, and even of new birth, or rebirth, Ishmael's plea underscores the price crewmembers pay: The eradication of wonder and awe, the ignoring of morals and the miraculous, for the momentary thrill of violence. The Pequod sails the open seas as a vessel of death, a time capsule of doom; the men on board, accomplices each and every one, must also perish. Ahab, the madman at its helm, must die. Starbuck, the moderate, will also perish. Pip and Queequeg will also die. Ishmael, the one who yearns to hold everyone's hand on board, in friendship, or in prayer, or something even more intimate, will, in the end, stare into the whirlpool of death, watching as it passes him by. He invites the miraculous, for in the end he favors life, hope, and the glimmer of renewal.

One wonders if, in 1850, those literary critics, reading Ishmael's provocative language, would have cringed, or laughed off the passage as silly, or worse, as mere parody? Or, could they have seen something profound in Ishmael's metaphysical conflation of pressing sperm oil and clasping hands, his temporary "insanity" an honest, forthright challenge to killing? Could they possibly have taken that passage as a yearning, a desire to banish forever all differences, an appeal to the universality of Ishmael's notion of "fellow-beings," and thus, and finally, an end to racial hatred and slavery—to lustful killing? Could they have conceived of an Ishmael transformed—done with killing, his urge for violence purged, involved in a ritual of renewal, of finding himself anew, what Dante called *retrovare*, a look back at the old self?

New Bedford had become home to Quakers, who dared not speak, obviously, of squeezing sperm, but who bent the arc of their conversations toward expressions of kindness, fairness, fellowship, and racial equality. The majority of Quakers, some of whom owned whaling vessels, were staunch abolitionists—many outspoken and active—which meant that some captains, in the whaling industry, at least, hired on free Blacks, enslaved Blacks, as well as those who had managed to rid themselves totally of their so-called masters. Frederick Douglass, freeing himself from enslavement and fleeing for freedom, worked on the docks in New Bedford, caulking whaling ships for his Quaker boss, and delivering speeches on abolition. At the same time, and in its own way, whaling helped finance the Atlantic slave trade. In a hard-to-believe calculus of the anti-human, spermaceti candles were exchanged in West Africa and the Caribbean for human cargo.

The vicious manner in which whalers pursued and tormented whales, binding them in ropes, then stabbing them with knives, sapping them of their will and determination, so that harpooners could begin the torture and the final kill, became a symbol of the slave trade and its maltreatment of West Africans. American slavers pursued and stole, tormented, wrapped in chains, and then sold as many able-bodied Africans that they could steal or kidnap or buy—humans as mere commodities—which meant, in far too many cases, their prolonged torment and torture unto death.

While almost all whales are either dark grey or black, Melville's mighty hunt flipped traditional expectations, for his is not simply lusting after the whitest of those creatures—Moby Dick—but for a whale so singular that it exists beyond color, its presence also a shocking absence, as it moves through the ocean without pigment. Such is that *avis rara*, the mysterious albino whale: Out of every 10,000 Sperm whales that will be born, only a single Moby Dick will swim beside them.

Melville's father-in-law was a principal figure maintaining slavery and segregation through the authority of federal law. Melville wanted Lemuel Shaw to see a rendering of equality, this one on the high seas, a camaraderie born of killing, but one that upended racism. And so Melville, an ungrateful son-in-law, threw a harpoon into the premiere Chief Justice of hate in the United States, who, for three decades, enshrined his belief in the inferiority of Black people into federal law, producing racist legislation that infected the country for far too many years.

The crew of the Pequod, men of many colors from various countries and religions—Zoroastrians, Native Americans, West Africans, South Sea Islanders, along with a few indentured whites, included the Polynesian Queequeg, the Quaker Starbuck, the African Daggoo, the African Americans Pip and Fleece, the Persian Fedallah, and the Gay Head Indian Tashtego—all of whom spent their hours and days, weeks, months, and on into two and three years, hunting down and killing one of nature's most majestic creatures. They lived an enforced, sometimes brutal closeness, beyond ethnicity and color, every movement kept in tight check by a ruthless captain and his endless regulations and rules, a stifling of freedom, ironically, creating a pale version of enslavement. But, there, on board ship, men ofen risked their lives for each other. Melville called them Isolatoes—"each living on a continent of his own"—solitary human beings of so many ethnicities that the decks of whaling ships became known, colloquially, as "checkerboards"—a distorted but nonetheless version of integration,

Indeed, Isolatoes were a strange turn of outcasts, who did not develop friendships easily, if at all, and who also distrusted the casual idea of camaraderie. Only the passion they had taken on for killing, only that most ruthless perversion, served as the foundation for their bonding. The crew of a whaler resembled a band of outlaws, on the run from themselves, united behind the butchering and sawing, the spiraling and rendering of fiercely alive creatures. If it resulted in profit, violence was justified.

Melville provided scenes of the worst details of death and torture, of men of all colors closed off to the pain they inflicted on other sentient creatures, ripping apart living beings, limb by limb, separating flesh from bone, organ from tissue, calf from cow. The reality is abhorrent; the result inexcusable—behavior beyond the human and certainly the humane. It was not just oil and blood that soaked deep into the deck of a whaler, but disgust and guilt. Aboard the Pequod, and on all other whalers, the idea of the civilized life must be rethought, revised, reconsidered and, for Melville, rewritten and recast.

The grotesqueries of violence shock, the behavior of men stings, the symbolism taunts and teases, the implications for this country's history of brutality against all living things stares back, haunts us, off the page and on the land. What happens to the essence of fiercely alive, magnificent creatures when placed under a regime of blind and callous slaughter, of unleashed butchery by an entire crew of men who have signed on as killers, as assassins, mesmerized by the lure of money? Slicing and sawing, the crew chanted their victories, like barbarians, maniacally taking life apart, bit by bit. Will they dismantle it all? Could they? On the open seas, where few can bear witness, limits get lifted, and the desire for more and more money strips people bare of their emotions and morals. The "1619 Project" informs us, or perhaps surprises us, that the slave trade in this country was negotiated on the open seas.

Barely thirty years old, Herman Melville was writing at the top of his lungs about an oncoming wave of greed so intense and distorted that it was capable of desecrating and destroying everything alive in not very much time at all; about a looming desire for wealth so intense, so out of control that people waged war on their most obvious and irreplaceable inheritance, on the natural world,in the hope of striking it rich.

Plantation owners, holy Puritans, believing in human beings as inspirited gifts from God, enslaved those they believed were markedly inferior, or who, in the evolutionary order, were radical mistakes—sports of creation—exploiting them to do the back-breaking work in the fields they refused to do themselves. In the 1850s, southern plantation owners listed, in approximate numbers, an astonishing four million West Africans held as chattel inventory.

Puritans had been whitewashed clean of sin, as befits the elect. To bend over in an undignified posture, hour after painful hour, in anything but prayer, was beyond imagining. To force their hands into dirt and muck insulted their sensibilities. Colonists, or rather Puritans, stood tall and erect, possessed of proper bearing, hands free of filth, hearts cleansed of sin. To dig in the Earth smacked too much of death. Those West Africans occupied some other, lesser category—non-human, black as sin, seared in Hell. They must be stopped from contaminating white families, which meant enslaving them, keeping them apart, and restricting them to the fields and their own shacks.

Such inhuman treatment of human beings laid a curse on the land and everything that grew on it: After all, it was sinners—sub-humans—who worked the fields, causing seeds to sprout and money to flow. Everything, all the crops and the land, but most especially the money, was tainted. On account of such exploitation of human beings, along with the accursedness of the land, itself, plantation owners had no qualms about disfiguring an Earth that was already polluted, thoroughly despoiled, and accursed. The "Raping of Mother Earth" is a metaphor that has far greater meaning than anything Freud might find in it.

Whaling thus made the insidious evil of slavery all the more apparent, for it thrived by sacrificing sentient beings—mammals aboard ship; mammals in the sea— for money. The whale was a resource, recalculated as a valuable commodity. Emerson visited New Bedford in 1833, with his Transparent Eyeball, and immediately shocked by one of the country's most lucrative enterprises: "Chasing the poor whale wherever he swims all round the globe, that they may tear off his warm jacket of blubber & melt it down into oil for your lamp, & to steal from him his bone to make stays and parasols for ladies."

To ensure the expansion of a capital economy, the Earth would have to be attacked with equal violence. Getting at its resources meant blasting off the tops of mountains, scraping them flat, boring deep inside the Earth's bowels, ripping out its innards, damming its streams and rivers and, if necessary, diverting their paths, slowly choking off the tumult of fish. Animal habitats would have to be bulldozed, which meant that not just a few, but entire species might have to be eradicated. All of it was done with total impunity, protected by law, and carried out in the name of necessity and progress. Once again: The siren-call of commerce—Money must be made. A handsome profit must be snatched from trafficking in the sheer and grotesque serial killing of whales.

Sperm whale oil could withstand the intense heat generated by those new machines, that demanded more and more of it in order to run at high-end speeds, permitting them to destroy with even greater efficiency. All of which meant the killing of more and more whales. As if out of some tall tale from the American South, those machines grew larger and mightier, their appetites greater, the tales more elaborate. Meanwhile, the Earth became some vast treasure chest in the belief that, no matter how much got extracted, it would replenish itself. Everything—values, morals, ethics, and life—were cast aside to satisfy those gargantuan machines. The dynamos simply had to remain dynamic.

In a most bizarre scenario, what those entrepreneurs extracted from the Earth—its coal, oil, and gas—was burned up as fuel, sending its poison into the atmosphere as carbon dioxide, methane, nitrous oxide, fluorinated gases, and more—as well as leaching poisons into the waterways and, as a consequence, even in the most remote places, forcing animals and plants to gasp for air and, finally, to suffocate. Those invisible, odorless, deadly gases persist in the atmosphere seemingly forever, holding in the heat, sending the temperature of the Earth ever higher, altering weather patterns, until conditions that support life became nearly unbearable, with plants, animals, and even fish unable to survive in a habitat critically ill with a high fever. It's impossible to recover from fires so intense that they explode, raging conflagrations with heat of such intensity they create their own winds, violent vortices of fire known as firewhirls, or fire whirlpools that scorch the Earth at 1,090 degrees Celsius, or 2,000 degrees Fahrenheit, the point at which aluminum melts.

People, without noticing it, began to inhabit an eerily quiet wasteland, and it took some time—perhaps too much time—before enough people began to notice and it took longer, still, before they were able to comprehend the catastrophe that they had visited on themselves, the horror they had to confront and attempt to repair. It took too long for enough people to notice and care and, finally, to shout: Enough! Everything is going to perish! By then, experts reported, most grimly, that it was too late, far too late even though someone like Keats had hinted at the horror of a cosmic hush before Melville and long before Rachel Carson: "The sedge has withered from the lake, /And no birds sing." Spring, indeed, had turned silent. What happened? People must ask: Just what happened to the birds, to spring, to the reality of renewal? When did April become "the cruellest month?"

And still, most people did not wake up to the poisoning of the Earth until far too many children were born with mysterious deformities, simply because their mothers had drunk tap water, from faucets in their own kitchens, that contained high concentrations of lead; until too many children were diagnosed with various kinds of cancer, from playing in fields contaminated with herbicides and pesticides. Most people did not grow angry until they fell ill eating fish from polluted lakes and streams; and not until entire families suddenly developed incurable skin irritations from swimming in childhood lakes, now polluted with tailings and toxic runoff.

They slowly woke up when they read that all the animals on the new factory farms had become sickened by unidentifiable infections, some so ill they required injections of a series of unpronounceable antibiotics to keep them alive long enough to be slaughtered as steaks and chops. They reeled at hearing of an outbreak, eerily named "Mad Cow's Disease," and found it unbelievable that ranchers were feeding so-called "downed cows" to those animals that were also ill but still standing.

What is Bovine Spongiform Encephalopathy, people wondered, that could lead to the unpronounceable Creutzfeldt-Jakob Disease, leaving people with no memory or vision? Why am I urinating antibiotics when I have not taken any? Why is there so much cancer of so many odd and unpronounceable kinds? Why do the medications all seem to trigger the most grotesque side effects? What remains that I can eat for lunch that is not poisonous? Who can I trust in a world where an algorithm makes decisions for me about my safety and well-being; where a robot answers the phone at almost every business; where the intellectual has been replaced by the influencer; where AI has kicked aside thinking? Life seems more and more designed for despair.

Melville is not merely dramatizing some whaling fiasco, fueled by outrage and revenge, under the command of a madman, but rather a drive, insatiable and unstoppable, of a new class of seemingly crazed and uncaring entrepreneurs—sociopaths disfigured by the demands of the new capital economy, with their outlandish behavior immunized by the law. Propelled into the future without ethical restraint, this new class was hell-bent on robbing every waterway, open field, deep wood, along with everything beneath the surface of the Earth, of its abundance, as if the entire planet had been put up for sale.

In the middle of the nineteenth century, Melville is after much more than an adventure on the sea, for he knew firsthand that the new land of equality and equity, of blistering opportunity, of a life renewed by religious freedom had become degraded by commerce, cursed by slavery, reserving freedom and success only for those with the correct skin color, ethnicity, and social rank. More and more became the cry, the demand, the plea, as the real world slowly disappeared. And so, the local general store made way for the grocery store, which led to the anonymity of the supermarket, and then buying online. Extraction and excavation were the easiest ways of getting at those endless natural riches, and enslaving men, women, and children the cheapest way to get the work done. There came to be many ways to enslave free souls and sell each one to people as one more step toward liberation and freedom.

After more than a century of men and their machines clawing and scraping, drilling, boring, and blasting, the phrase *natural resource*, in 1956, finally forced its way into the language, creating the fiction that no treasure deep inside the Earth, or on land or water, could ever run out because, by definition, a *resource* had the power, like that miraculous gadget in the fairy tale, "The Magic Porridge Pot," to re-source itself.

Just seven short years later, in 1963, the British author, Aldous Huxley, who had emigrated to America in the thirties, countered that idea of nature's unending riches by publishing *The Politics of Ecology: The Question of Survival,* in which he considers the word *ecology*—from Greek *oikos,* or "home"—warning that corporations were fast depleting the Earth of its limited resources. Humanists like Huxley and Carson, and not the long list of scientists, began to reveal the truth: Human beings, relying on pesticides, herbicides, and avicides were poisoning the food they ate, the water they drank, the air they breathed, and the planet on which they lived.

As early as 1963, then, Aldous Huxley stood up for the survival of the Earth: "Only when we get it into our collective head that the basic problem confronting twentieth-century man [sic] is an ecological one will our politics improve and become realistic." Those who exploited the Earth knew the eventual cost and seemed not to care a whit. Money had made them blind and deaf; profit made them dumb: They had become the architects of their own demise. Slowly, but most assuredly, the so-called climate scientists began to worry about the possibility of our wholesale eviction from the planet, itself, prefiguring the demise of our *oikos.*

Melville foresaw a good deal of that ecological horror a full century before it became apparent, especially to the majority of climate scientists. He knew well its origins up close and in detail, and saw that once they were set in motion, such a catastrophe could never be stopped. On the horizon appeared what can be called, accurately, the Grand Removal—which marketing wizards sold to the public as Mother Nature generously giving over, offering to us all her unending abundance.

In the midst of the climate catastrophe, scientists promised a paradise where, in the new future, using cutting-edge technology, they would redesign life through gene editing, creating a world free of disease, with death little more than a nuisance: The centi-billionaires, most of them who came to larger-than-life in the Silicon Valley, demanded nothing short of eternal life. They deserved it, for with AI they had broken the intelligence barrier. Those who viewed intelligence, indeed, as something artificial, or mechanical, favored the wonders of a life without the need for thinking, opting for the thrill of a machine that could calculate and that needed little beyond periodic repair, additional memory, and a bit of oiling.

Nature cannot be improved. It can only be destroyed. Waves kiss the shore, retreat to the open sea and, in their eternal return, suck up more and more of the shoreline. Against such powerful tsunamis of incoming prosperity, in Melville's calculation, a movement in the opposite direction, an undertow of destruction and death, was taking place without anyone noticing. The figment of progress is countered by the grim reality of degradation. In the fall of 1851, with the arrival of *Moby Dick*, a great many people in this country were riding high on a wave of enthusiasm about the advent of the new machine age.

It was that backwash, that riptide of madness, that Melville understood so deeply, which made itself obvious in the grotesquerie called whaling, the most horrific and premeditated carnage carried out in the far reaches of every one of the oceans in the world. The inflow of money must always be countered, to return to the wisdom of Oceanica, by an inevitable undertow that takes out with it the essential imperatives that make living authentic and enviable—those twins called ethics and morality. With every stab he made into the flesh of the whale, a crewmember lost another piece of his humanity.

For whales do not just live in this world, cavorting in the depths of the oceans. They romp and play and fascinate as biblical kin, as primal ancestors in the chain of being. And, with their pedigree founded in Genesis, they swim in the oceans of the world as Ur-creatures, as the first of all firsts, and in mighty and near unbelievable ways. While those two primal beings—whales and humans—enjoy separate domains, it is human beings who break into their homes and rob them of their lives.

On the fifth day of Creation, in Genesis, sentient life does not appear where we might most reasonably expect it, on land and in plain view—a miracle for all to admire (or envy). Rather, life begins where we must have faith that it exists, deep in the deepest oceans. There, life takes hold—another surprise—not with some average-sized being, but with creatures so immense they challenge belief, itself. Thus, life begins larger than so-called life-size, with those over-sized leviathans.

Given the primal importance of the whale, Melville dramatizes, with gruesome detail, the wicked annihilation of not just one of the most miraculous, muscular and surprising creatures in the world, but God's first sentient creation, whale or leviathan, which, to repeat, came into the created world at the close of Day Five or, as the inspired Melville has it, in his prose that can elevate to the edge of heaven: "Leviathan comes floundering down upon us from the head-waters of the Eternities . . . "

The King James Version of Genesis, 1:20-23, describes that "floundering down," an image which sneaks in a fish: "And God said, Let the waters bring forth abundantly the moving creation that hath life, and fowl may fly above the Earth in the open firmament of heaven. And God created great whales, and every living creature that moveth, which the waters brought forth abundantly, after their kind, and every winged fowl after his kind: and God saw that *it was good*. And God blessed them, saying, be fruitful, and multiply, and fill the waters in the seas, and let fowl multiply in the Earth. And the evening and the morning were the fifth day." Not until two days later does the human being, Adam, assume his first breath, making his appearance, which should be astonishing, as a conclusion, of sorts, to the rest of creation, but which pales before the descriptions of wilder life in nature.

An amalgam of fish and mammal, of scales and hair, dorsal fins and retractable nipples, of lethargy and colossal strength, whales demonstrate great care and concern for their calves, as well as for other whales in distress. Calves are born tail-first, so the cold water can harden their tails and fins, for they must swim, immediately, to the surface to take their first breath of air. Mature whales move through the water with bisected tail and fore-limbs, some species displaying ferocious looking teeth. Males can weigh upwards of 30,000 pounds, and females, weighing 10,000 pounds, have mammary slits, retractable nipples, and can produce milk thick enough to be propelled, deep underwater, into the mouth of its calf, which remains close to its mother for an astonishing ten years or so, before it swims off on its own. When stimulated by the calf's nudges, the nipples emerge and the feeding begins.

Even with their enormous weight, because whales have lungs, they must periodically erupt from deep in the ocean for air, leaping ten to fifteen feet straight up in a spectacle called breaching. For whales, sound is their strongest sense, allowing them to participate in long-distance choral arrangements that serve as messages about locations of food and the condition of other whales. Or, they sing for pleasure: A song that might start in the Atlantic undergoes an astounding journey— passing from whale to whale—finally reaching the Pacific where whales hear them, causing them to alter their original songs. Whales are thus particularly affected by the Navy sonar and the so-called "air-bombs" that riggers explode under water to locate oil deposits. Fourteen Cuvier's beaked whales beached in the Bahamas, blood pouring from their ears, a result of having to swim to the surface too quickly to escape high-pitched sonar. As the 2018 documentary, "Sonic Sea" so graphically shows, they suffered from their own version of "the bends," their bleeding the result of brain hemorrhaging.

Although far outweighing the shark, whales glide through the water at an astonishing thirty miles per hour. Unlike sharks, whales never lurk, circle, and attack the unsuspecting, much preferring to play and eat. Four stomachs give the Sperm whale a voracious appetite, requiring three tons of shrimp a day, a meal made easier to ingest given a pair of eighteen-foot jaws. They also exhibit sexual dimorphism, possess the largest brain of any species, weighing up to twenty pounds, five times more than humans. The animal gets its name from the spermaceti organ in its head that holds nearly 500 gallons of oil. In interludes of about fifteen minutes, Sperm whales sleep without moving or breathing, totally upright, one eye open and the other closed, the same posture they use for breaching. Whales have a body temperature of 100 degrees Fahrenheit. Blue whales, among the largest creatures ever recorded, reach 100 feet long, and weigh over 400,000 pounds.

The spark of all biblical life begins where no human could ever hope to survive. Life begins where no person can even bear eyewitness, but must have faith that creation thrives there in a most miraculous way, that it flourishes out of sight and beyond our control. At the underwater shelf of the Earth, at depths unimaginable, there complexity and beauty thrive, whales leap and lounge, give birth and nurse, and provide lessons for our own land-locked beings. The great chain of discovery admits of no vacancies. In seemingly blind alleys, life abounds. It is little wonder that the Anglo-Saxon kenning for the ocean, *hron-rade*, translates as "whale-road."

Nature simply does not need us, or our notions of improvement and efficiency, in order to flourish. The invitation nature sends is not to control and direct, but to witness and wonder, to delight and marvel. We have been prepared to approach the world with awe. We need the invigoration that only nature can provide, an expression that both Plato and Aristotle found in a single word, *thaumazein*, and which served as the definition of philosophy: "The wonder at all that is, as it is." It is an attitude that ought to begin, for us, with the leviathans. Which might explain why Ahab is so determined to see them hacked apart, for he yearns to destroy at the most fundamental, religious level, in which such an act of killing, of such basic retaliation, makes him feel powerful, like a creator perverted.

Whaling began in this country in the seventeenth century, expanding rapidly and, following the trajectory of the Industrial Revolution, exploding in the middle of the nineteenth century. Shipping records from 1829 show that the three major ports—New Bedford, Nantucket, and New London—had a total of 203 whaling ships registered. Five years later, in 1834, that number had more than doubled, to 421. By 1840, out of a total of 900 whaling ships registered world-wide, New England accounted for more than eighty percent, or 735 ships. By 1850, behind textiles, coal, cotton, and railroads, whaling ranked number five. In terms of adventure and romance, whaling came first.

Ishmael describes killing aboard ship as gruesome, as acts of murder, but in his earliest days, he found it exotic and thrilling, gigantic corpses whose girth got measured in dollars. Early in the narrative, as he wanders the streets of New Bedford, Ishmael realizes how such a small, remote place became the center of wealth: "Go and gaze upon the iron emblematical harpoons round yonder mansions, and your question will be answered. Yes, all those brave houses and flowering gardens came from the Atlantic, Pacific, and Indian Oceans. One and all, they were harpooned and dragged up hither from the bottom of the sea." In 1854, New Bedford, with a population of 20,000, had the highest per capita income of any place in the country. Whaling created fortunes; killing helped to build mansions. *Forbes* magazine calls the wealth that resulted in Macy's, General Motors, Hathaway Textiles and thus and eventually with Warren Buffet, as "Blubber Capitalism."

In a single year, 1853, whalers killed a staggering 8,000 whales, rendered into 103,000 barrels of sperm oil, 260,00 barrels of whale oil, and 5.7 million pounds of baleen, enough death to produce $11 million or, in 2022 figures, a staggering $408,000,000 in profit. Those whales ended up as oil for cooking, lighting, and lubrication; as baleen for corsets, buggy whips, umbrella arms, and fishing rods; as ambergris for perfume; and later, as sushi and pet food.

Killing in such obscene numbers recalls that phrase of finality, *human-created extinction*, or what Rachel Carson called *biocide*. Which, again, might make a deranged captain feel as if he possessed the power of some mighty god, able to decide with a single command and several harpoons what shall live and what must die. Killing, on a grand scale, began in earnest in the ocean, followed quickily and most methodically by the decimation of the Earth.

To know the wondrous nature of the whale, facing off against a band of entrepreneurs determined to hack and carve it into mere commodities, is to realize Melville's fears about the fate of the natural world under the assault of an expanding capital economy which, even in its incipient stage, and before it got named *capitalism*, in 1854, in William Thackeray's novel, *The Newcomes,* thrived on killing. If the Earth was to be rescued, such devastation had to be stopped immediately.

A captain is sailing maniacally on the skin of those primeval oceans, and he is navigating his ship in and among the hugest of primeval creatures—for he is the master of his floating microcosm—and he is called Ahab, named for a ferocious king, in the Book of Kings. That King, and this Captain, both serve as warnings: Ahab stands in for those arrogant captains of industry who, in the next century, will wreak havoc on land, plot by plot, species by species, creating their mayhem in the pursuit of oil. Ahab embodies that ragged emotion, rage, so essential for the goals called progress and development, and so revealing of their destructive force. Rage befits him, for he is a universal villain, a ferociously alive warning about the vengeance that humanity is capable of wreaking on the smallest to the largest creatures, from the first and startlingly magnificent of them to the very least and last.

Driving that killing is oil, first rendered from whales, then hacked out of rocks, and extracted with machinic violence from deep within the Earth. Like rabid addicts, people craved oil in staggering, unlimited amounts, burning it, and thus turning it into a poison, killing off everything sentient and alert, no matter the cost to the living, for huge profits were at stake. To attack the Earth with such lethality, and without a single cringe, revealed that the heart of nature had been denatured, disenchanted, fallen to something less than sacred, no longer speaking the language of its Creator. Indeed, language had become semantically inert. Melville intended to re-enchant our habitat. He began with a call for naming and renaming with the clarity and power of Adam.

Absent his conscience, Ahab knows a desire that far outstrips even the extreme limits of greed, believing that the world would be better if he were God, or one of the gods, powerful enough to decide what and who should be permitted to live. His role would be assured if he could wipe out God's authority by destroying those primal creatures. In Ahab's warped view, creation can only be topped with acts so startling they reek of de-creation. For Ahab, his rage against that one white and resistant creature has transported him beyond the wealth of whale oil and bone, and far beyond blubber. Ahab has been wronged, his presumption interrupted, and by nothing less than a dumb animal. Such is the nature of insult to the arrogant. And, he has been most certainly wounded, in flesh and psyche, and the guiltiest of the whales must pay the highest price.

Keep in mind that Ahab is a sanctioned killer with a reputation for turning living things into hefty profits. Banks underwrite him, investors cheer him on, merchants rely on his skill at bringing back the kill. Given permission, he could eradicate the entire population of whales: He has vengeance and the law on his side. Such arrogance has no limits and once set in motion, such lust will destroy everything. But as captain, in charge of the rules, Ahab's rage must extend well beyond all that is logical or reasonable. Inspired by its classical incarnation, his raging, or outraging has been supercharged with the charge of pure ego. Ahab cannot be contained—not easily, perhaps not at all.

In Melville's hands, that wicked Israelite becomes a sea-going madman bent on destroying well beyond our understanding, for he possesses a vision that reduces the miracle of the whale into something ferocious, mean-spirited, and evil, a most devious enemy. For the greater good of society, and for Ahab's own sense of the ancient law of *lex talionis*, "retaliation," or "getting even"—an eye for eye, a tooth for a tooth—Moby Dick must surrender its life.

Ahab goes up against more than just the authority of the bible. He takes on God by attacking the whale and the place that it holds in the biblical scheme of creation, making the pursuit of Moby Dick an assault against creation, itself, and thus against all living things. Killing at such a basic level must count as an Ur-disaster, a dismantling of Earth's magnificence, destruction that accelerated and expanded, that swelled well beyond understanding and apology. In the end, staring into the grim face of destruction, we must become more than outraged.

By its very own distortions and exaggerations, by the stupendous size of its antagonist, by the significance of several of its biblical characters, underscored by its tough and dense language, *Moby Dick* depicts a reality, up close and in full view, that has been picked apart and destroyed by an entrepreneurial regime gone mad with lust and made legitimate by law, determined, not simply or merely to destroy, but to extinguish virtually everything that lives. All this, we must keep in mind, was done, not merely or only for some perverse joy or pleasure, but also for a fairly recent and thrilling enticement, an elusive but most thrilling goal called profit.

On August 27, 1859, what has been called "the most important well ever drilled" began belching oil, in the remote town of Titusville, Pennsylvania. Whalers could render a total of 4,000 barrels of whale oil over three years. In a single day, the Titusville well delivered 3,000 barrels of oil. Such a discovery on land, one might imagine, should have put a damper on the killing of whales, but the killing of whales had become something of a routine and slowed not at all. In 1858, one year before Titusville, as if whalers knew that petroleum might put an to end their enterprise, harpooners, astonishingly, killed more whales than in any other single year.

Nearly forty years after the gusher at Titusville, in 1895, fifty-one whaling vessels still departed from four ports in New England. The International Whaling Commission did not outlaw whaling until nearly one hundred years later, in 1986. The commercial killing of whales settled slowly into a grotesque routine of serial assassinations that went mostly unreported. An enormous Blue whale, the largest animal ever to have lived, weighing as much as forty elephants, hung from the ceiling of the Natural History Museum, a corrupted trophy commemorating this nation's industrial devotion to outright, unregulated slaughter of nature's most magnificent sentient beings.

Melville brings readers to an up-close, magnified view of killing—in the very bloodiest, most intensely cruel and shuddering details of hunting and hectoring; of men, in abandon, yelling and thrusting harpoon after harpoon into the resistant flesh of highly sentient creatures. "Die," they might be yelling, "Die now!" First, the stabbing with harpoons, then the decapitation with lances, followed by the slicing with razor-sharp knives, and then the spurting, the awful geysers of blood. Rage and hate, and the prospect of money, made slicing hunks of flesh off those behemoths necessary and even for those on deck, fun. In the end, the crew rejoiced in the swabbing of the "greasy decks," thick with blood, oil, and guts.

In his blown-up horror that was whaling, Melville forced readers to confront the reality of the whale as a preternaturally outlandish mammal—as one of us but vastly different from us—as a creature alive beyond any easy definition, close to unbelievable and simply unable to be contained by the usual boundaries or definitions. Melville moves us, swiftly, past the commercial to the anger and rage needed to carry out the ruthless ending of so much sentient, magnificent life.

He makes us wonder about all the planning, the financing, the felling of trees needed for building those ships, and the recruiting of men for a nefarious enterprise that operated out of sight and beyond oversight. In reading Melville, we catch ourselves eavesdropping on acts of violence that over the years confronted nature with such arrogance it forced an unbelievable number of animals and their habitats into extinction, gone forever, and utterly, totally forgotten. What should we call eradication on such a scale? Such levels of horror drove Melville, first, to the bible to resurrect religious categories of hate and malignity, and then to the *Iliad* for Classical accounts of rage and outrage, and back, once more, to the ocean he so loved to save the sanctity of life.

Ishmael tells us what has happened, some time after the story has essentially ended, after the Pequod has sunk and the crew drowned, leaving him as our storyline, who has been treading water, for two days, up to his neck and making us into his lifeline. Until his rescue, he will take us back to the beginning of the voyage, and ahead to the moment when Moby Dick throws off its harpoons, turns on its attacker, and smashes its massive body into the Pequod, demolishing wood and flesh, the inert and the living.

There is never a retailing of events in the present, not even at the very end, for as Ishmael informs us in the Postscript, he has been "picked up at last." Melville leaves us with a rough image of our own plight, of wreaking havoc on the natural world and of nature in utter revolt. It is an image that remains biblical, marked with floods and droughts, ice and fire, with an unbelievable number of species of fauna and flora driven into extinction. We are left wondering, has that fictional, biblical catastrophe, *Moby Dick,* become our reality?

The grand assault against life began with the denigration, if not of a religious sense of the created world, then with the loss of a sacred or even majestic idea of nature, the ancient attitude of wonder at all things as they are, replaced by something approaching the thrill of amassing huge profits from all things as they are commodities. With that first gusher, money trumped magnificence, a moment of jubilation for investors, and a sheer disaster for the Earth and all things dependent on clean air. As the drive after fossil fuels ramped up, it meant the amassing of fortunes, and spelled the end for everything else.

In December 1976, a tanker named the Argo Merchant, loaded with 7.7 million gallons of oil, ran aground near the dangerous Nantucket shoals, off the coast of Massachusetts. Two days later, it broke in half and sank, resulting in the world's first major oil spill: a pool of toxic sludge covering an area of 69 by 115 miles. Winds carried it out into the open seas, where the sludge slowly sank, poisoning life out of view, silently and invisibly. Oil was first harvested from the ocean, from Sperm whales, then on land with the extraction of tar, and then, ironically and tragically, through far too many spills, oil moved back to the high seas as a death sentence to marine life. The Argo became the worst disaster imaginable.

That is, until a bit more than ten years later, on March 24, 1989, when the supertanker christened the Valdez, owned by Exxon Oil, ran aground on the Bligh Reef off the coast of Alaska, resulting in the worst oil disaster in history. According to the Exxon Valdez Oil Spill Trustee Council, over the next few days, as the ship began to break apart, it spilled a whopping 10.8 million gallons of crude oil into the Prince William Sound, spreading its toxic tar over 1,500 miles of the Gulf of Alaska, killing 250,000 seabirds, 2,800 sea otters, 300 harbor seals, 250 bald eagles, and some 22 killer whales. Exxon appealed its more than 30,000 class actions to the Supreme Court and, citing laws that had been promulgated by Melville's father-in-law, managed to have the 2.5-billion-dollar settlement vacated, reducing damages to 500 million. If they wanted to continue their lifestyles, people would just have to live with the poisoning of a most generous portion of nature. (In 2007, it took Exxon Mobil only two days of the first quarter to produce revenue of 2.5 billion dollars.)

Melville describes nature de-natured. He knows, he warns, and he tries, with all his writing might, to send up a warning. The maniacal Ahab, deranged biblical king, a character bordering on caricature, king of all killing, flailing and fuming, raging and railing, is emblematic of the deranged mania for wealth that began to infect entrepreneurs in the middle of the nineteenth century. He is possessed of a diabolical hatred intensified with a fury that rages beyond all limits, with a goal, unspoken, of emptying the Earth—looting on the grandest scale imaginable—of all its contents for nothing other than money—obscene amounts of money. While the Earth's bounty remains finite, investment must expand, profits must increase—limits must be eliminated. Entrepreneurs eventually run out of riches, digging and dynamiting no longer yielding a profit, investment ending in frustration and anger in corporate boardrooms. Greed blinds people to the truth, insinuating itself like some untreatable infection, weakening people's resolve. So seductive is the promise of power and infinite potential of a capital economy, few people have the insight to see it for what it is—a highly infectious virus, with fewer willing or able to stop its inexorable contagion.

In those earliest years, as we know only too well, few if any people actually read *Moby Dick* and the great majority of those who could read it, or should have read it, went on in their occluded way, ignoring its underlying meaning, choosing to see it as a morality tale, a protracted chase to eliminate an obstinate, offensive creature. That time has vanished. In this, our catastrophic climate we must heed Herman Melville, for he foresaw what nobody could have predicted—the end of nature.

If we are to save this home, this *oikos* and its extension, *ecology*, then we must take heed and take action. We must ask, what to do, and what can we do, and how can we repair this assault against the environment that has now become so blatantly, so forcefully the grimmest of all catastrophes. Change is no longer simply necessary; it is no longer something that we will get around to. It is crucial and it is critical. Behind our power to verbalize is our ability to think, to hatch ideas, and thus to effect change. We have the ability to bring something new into the world, to create and re-create. That is something wondrous.

Nature has had enough, hurling itself, in revolt, against our own ship of state, which now threatens to splinter into pieces. How should we begin; where must we begin; what must we repair and forego before all else and anything else? We must think, and then change our own minds. We must reorder our priorities, repair our attitudes, and realign our interests. The most immediate and most effective fix lies nowhere else but within each of us.

In any case, we have little time to save what remains of the natural world. That same Sixth UN Assessment of the Condition of the Climate warns that we have moved dangerously close to the point of no return. If we do not radically reduce our levels of greenhouse gases, life on Earth will struggle and stumble for perhaps thirty more years. Such a conclusion, from such an august body is, to say the least, shocking. Global warming must be held fast at 1.5 degrees Celsius above pre-industrial times. Can we turn aside our suicide mission? Can we be content without the power to control? Is it too late? Is the killing of nature just too much with us?

In *Moby Dick*, Melville has presented us with a Manifesto that, in its demand not just to be read but to be acted upon, insists that we dispense with the known and the usual. Instead of destroying, we must embrace the myriad living things of the natural world, learn the many ways of caring for nature, embrace the natural as sacred and wondrous. All of which demands from each of us something enormous: We must dispense with the idea that, in order to feel alive and alert, we have to destroy in order to consume, and in order to feel fully satisfied we need to consume more and more and even more.

Moby Dick makes itself known through something more significant than its outsized limits. We know it most potently by its ability, not only to outwit Ahab, but to destroy him, and return (or escape) back to the sanctity under the sea, where it can no longer be seen, back to its beginnings in the depths of creation. We embrace Moby Dick for the wonder of the innate and the natural. To kill that creature for profit, to slice it into parts, is a corruption beyond reckoning, a violation beyond imagining, a perversion well beyond forgiveness.

Moby Dick swims off as victor but not victorious, a creature hounded and wounded, a behemoth entangled in whaling's web of thick ropes, sharpened harpoons, and perverted philosophy—even in its freedom, the humiliation of industrial death hangs on, glories in its traces. Moby Dick may have escaped the madness of humans, but for how long? For there are scores of other whalers, in a madness that denigrates all sentient life, who are eager to kill, and, especially, to kill the largest whales imaginable.

Melville does not answer that most essential question—how can we learn to leave nature alone?—but he knows that it demands a response. He leaves us to wonder what to do, and what must be done, because the answer lies within the independent being of each of us. The question must thus stimulate each one of us into action. It can, and it must. For the unfolding of Melville's narrative is obviously not a tale of victory, but a study in undoing, and the critical need for restoration.

Moby Dick indicts. Reading to the end, we simply cannot feel satisfied, as we do after great reading experiences, for we have faced the unimaginable, near inconceivable—a harpoon in the heart of our being. Again, although Moby Dick has fled, it has been chased, harassed, molested, harpooned, wounded, and scarred; it has also been quite literally entangled in the web of civilization. Can Moby Dick ever recapture the purity of being whale, qua whale, again? For while Moby Dick may be free, it has met a madness from those creatures who live on land head-on, an insistence to kill and consume all things ordinary and extraordinary.

In this telling and on this voyage, there can be no winners, there can be no satisfying conclusion, not a hint of closure—only more pondering and puzzlement. And thus, Melville's narrative cannot conclude but must sail on to its final page, the future occluded, satisfaction and justice postponed. We will keep turning the pages until Ishmael runs out of breath, or until we run out of patience. No, we are not done, for we have yet to read the Epilogue—only then can we put the book down and say, "I have read it, word-for-word, from cover-to-cover." Only then does the action truly begin, and the plotting truly start, no longer prompted by the author, but passed on to the reader—the way responsibility ought to shift in a manifesto, from writer to reader, from author to authority, from what fell apart to how to repair it.

In the end, is the reader, like Ishamel, as the last word of the Epilogue puts it, an *orphan?* Ishmael called on us to grant him a name, to bestow on him an identity, and now he clams up, sails out of sight, and leaves us baffled. The biblical Ishmael is not exactly an orphan, but something closer to the Greek *orphos,* a state of "being deprived," no longer a citizen of a place, but uprooted and homeless.

"Call Me Friend," we want to shout after him, for in our own moral confusion, we, too, feel deprived, orphaned without a good-bye or a proper thanks: "It was the devious-cruising Rachel, that in her retracing search after her missing children, only found another orphan." Perhaps all we can expect in our own voyage is to set sail, every last one of us, as orphans—displaced, outcast, and down-cast. Melville forces us to confront something basic: In this, the most advanced civilization, are we deprived, and in the most fundamental way, cast out and exiled from true dwelling? Have we been robbed of that most fundamental *privilege*—to know life as wondrous? For the idea of *orphan* implies that we have lost the gift of intimacy with an infinitude of creatures and plants, lost the language of knowing with every seed and spore. Orphaned and estranged, we have severed our lifeline with all things wild, ending up in a wilderness of our own making.

Like Ishmael, we are set adrift, waiting for someone or something to rescue us, in desperate need of being reunited with nature, both human and other. Dislocated, we are no longer able to think and act, no longer certain how we should feel or, in some abstract way, how we might even feel. The unbalancing of nature has taken its toll. We have been duped and abandoned, estranged by seeming success, orphaned by obvious excess.

Entrepreneurs claimed the Earth as theirs for the taking, blinded by money-making schemes and embued with a solemn duty—they believed—to take advantage of it all. Who owns the ocean? At any one moment, it is Ahab, or it is Captain Gardiner, or one of the thousands of other whalers. Who owns the land? It must be the entrepreneur. Such are the distortions in the arc of American history, not of the abuses of politics and power, but of the devastation of companies and corporations. Such is the grim reality that hides behind a string of stupefying nouns, like progress, speed, efficiency, inclusion, eminent domain, Indian removal, and ease of living for (nearly) all. What is missing is another string of contrary nouns, verbs, and adjectives, like destruction, devastation, killing, looting, demolishing, and poisoning.

In Melville's forecasting of such a degraded world, the whale fell from a being of utter magnificence to a great source of money, its blubber, bone, and oil, a cache of outsized profits. Because it seemed such a devilish creature; because it lived, unseen, in the vastness of some ocean; because whalers risked their lives for the kill, whaling companies felt justified in demanding high prices for bringing home the loot. Whale oil, itself, screamed of a luxury that emphasized pure *lux*, recalling the command and keeping its connection with the bible on the first day: "Let there be Light!"

For the most agile and persistent of entrepreneurs, those willing to exploit the Earth's so-called natural resources, no matter the cost, there was money to be harvested out of a vast body of water that belonged to no one. Every fish that moved, every whale that blew off steam, every plant and piece of seaweed and coral, carried a price tag. The ocean meant wave upon wave of unending profit, with no license needed for extinguishing an entire species, for no one policed the seas. And, after removing the ocean's treasures, those same entrepreneurs could then use that same ocean, in a most nasty arrangement, as their giant waste receptacle.

Whaling was a huge industry, needing great investment. The Charles W. Morgan whaler, built in New Bedford, in 1841, required a small forest to build its

106-foot hull, which consumed 50,000 board-feet of live oak, along with a variety of other woods for its compartments, decks, and triple mast, rising 110 feet. (A 2,000 square-foot house requires around 16,000 board-feet of lumber, or approximately twenty-two mature pine trees. The Morgan caused close to seventy mature Oak Trees to be felled.) The Morgan cost $27,000 to build, close to $52,786 fully outfitted, or today, upwards of $800,000. It carried a crew of thirty-five, along with four whaling boats, each over twenty-five feet long.

With its initial launch, on September 6, 1841, the Morgan joined the seventy-five other whalers that left New England ports, and did not complete the last of its thirty-seven voyages until some eighty years later, in the fall of 1920. Most whalers could remain at sea for about three years, but since the Morgan had its own fire pits, called "trypots," the crew not only rendered whale fat on board, but also stored it for long periods of time, making it possible for the Morgan to remain at sea for five or six years. The crew was forbidden to eat the local fish because the copper sheathing on the hull leached salts and poisoned sea life. On the Morgan's initial voyage, which lasted four years, the ship's log records fifty-nine whales killed, rendered into 1,600 barrels of sperm oil, 800 barrels of right whale oil, as well as an unbelievable 10,000 pounds of whale bones. Such carnage resulted in a profit of $53,000, or today, $750,000.

From 1841 to 1921, the Charles A. Morgan logged 437 voyages around the world, killing over 4,000 whales, rendered into 54,483 barrels of sperm and whale oil; 152,934 pounds of bones; and, out of all that death and gore, a profit, in 2023 equivalent, of close to $16 million. The whale, a creature that very few people ever saw, was America's principle natural resource, and its oil one of its most lucrative products. What does an economy based on killing and enslavement do to the nature of a country, to its sense of its accomplishments, to its need to hide a history that is already, and ironically, out of view?

Whaling began in New England, in the 1790s, some thirty years before the first gold nugget was hacked out of the Earth in Georgia, and close to sixty years before the great rush in California. It reached its peak in 1857, with New Bedford alone registering 329 vessels, and employing some 10,000 men. Twenty other ports were also active. There is no telling how many million whales those whaling vessels, over their protracted lifetimes, harassed to exhaustion, tortured, and finally killed. The whaling industry, to repeat, destroyed life far out of view, so that few people could ever imagine its gruesome details, or the long-range, unsettling effects of its sustained killing.

Melville let them know those details. He describes whalers leaving the port of Nantucket for the wildness of the open seas, his sentences demanding a careful reading, as they reveal his indictment of willful, irresistible killing by men no longer earth-dwellers, no longer bound by its customs and rules:

> "The Nantucketer, he alone resides and riots on the sea . . . *There* is his home; *there* lies his business, which a Noah's flood would not interrupt though it over-whelmed all the millions in China. He lives on the sea, as prairie cocks in the prairie; he hides among

the waves, he climbs them as chamois hunters climb the Alps. For years he knows not the land; so that when he comes to it at last, it smells like another world, more strangely than the moon would to an Englishman. With the landless gull, that at sunset folds her wings and is rocked to sleep between billows; so, at nightfall, the Nantucketer, out of sight of land, furls his sails, and lays him to his rest, while under his very pillow rush herds of walruses and whales."

It is one thing to fall asleep while dreaming of a herd of whales and walruses swimming beneath one's bunk, but Melville makes us wonder about the innocence of that dream: What rushes under the whaler's head is money.

By writing about the whale, the largest creature in nature, Melville provokes us to wonder about the nature of all nature: What is it that inheres in every animal, in each creature, no matter size or shape; what is it that shocks and surprises; that will startle a person, finally, into taking delight in its very astonishing and complex character, with its most miraculous and mysterious ways of being—and, in the most unusual case of the whale, with a being that remains so much out of sight? It is difficult to imagine what could prompt, let alone encourage, such ferocious killing. Only money, it seems, and ever more amounts of money, could override all moral, ethical, or religious injunctions against such a transgressive act. Greed is a most potent anaesthetic.

If we hope to rescue life on this planet, we must abandon such blind and arrogant violence, and see that every single creature, every ant and tick that we swat aside, each tiny or large animal we crush to death, is possessed of its own wondrous nature, which it displays in its own particular and peculiar way. All things—even that tiny menace, the mosquito, can delight and startle with its intricate, calibrated behavior.

We have no right, no license, and certainly no authority to snuff out sentient life. All creatures possess their own tier of complicated being and all of them—each and every one of them—deserves to live out its destiny. This must be evident without anyone declaring some creature dangerous and in need of euthanization. Why do we have to insist that all living things be treated with respect in order for the world to continue? It is astonishing but true.

Melville foresaw a regime of killing without regret or penalty, one most eager to exploit all of nature, holding nothing sacred. To get at that treasure-chest it became necessary to tear open the fabric of the Earth, with violence—gouging the land while poisoning the waters. In the exploding boon of life as innovation and comfort, the word *destruction* must never be uttered, the word *exploitation* never invoked, and the word *profit* never mentioned. Instead, speak of *exploration* and *progress, of efficiency* and *comfort*, and of the *lush* and the *luxurious*.

Once set in motion, such a perverse attitude toward the land and its living creatures could never be stopped, only exacerbated, as nature became not simply a source of enormous wealth, but a receptacle for the waste that mining, digging, fracking, and dynamiting—the so-called refining of fossil fuels—inevitably produced. Giant corporations knew that their tailings were highly toxic, non-biodegradable, and radioactive, making them lethal for centuries, but still they dumped it all in streams, rivers, lakes, and in the oceans. After all, water was for flushing.

We were led to believe that corporate explorers and miners, almost by definition, were not to blame—they needed to dispose of their deadly waste, since death always nips at the heels of progress. And, besides, did we not, like the honey-colored whale oil in the past, need the new coal-black kind to ensure our progress? That magical place, once again out of view, where huge corporations, along with individual families, throw their garbage "away" is not merely an illusion, but a perverse one. The belief in an unending receptacle is merely the opposite fantasy of the never-ending natural resource. In reality, toxic garbage ends up in the deepest recesses of the forests, and in the farthest reaches of the oceans of the world, choking off life. Where Ishmael once clutched his coffin, huge islands of plastic now turn in circles. The Pacific Garbage Patch, an unbelievable 1.6 million square kilometers, floats between Hawaii and California, while another revolves in the North Atlantic.

Our current world is the product of self-deception and a blind belief in the beneficence of corporations and their products. The delusion of recycling provides a good example: People cinch the strings on their green garbage bags and drop them inside their green cans, believing that their trash will be recycled, reborn in some other form, and feeling a bit virtuous for having done their part in the cycle of recycling. But, behind all those forest-green promises, a yellow light flashes caution: Other countries have begun to refuse our refuse, making our landfills overflow, releasing extreme amounts of methane, a potent greenhouse gas that persists in the atmosphere for over one hundred years, forty times longer than CO_2. In 2020, the EPA estimated that yearly methane emissions from landfills equalled the CO_2 from 20,000,000 cars running day and night, all year. In 2022, this country managed to export over 950 million pounds of plastic scrap to five countries: Canada, Mexico. Malaysia, Indonesia, and Vietnam.

The recycling industry solved its horror of getting rid of far too much non-biodegradable waste by dumping it in the oceans, the poisonous cargo drifting over the horizon, out of sight, out of mind, and far beyond the reach of anyone's responsibility. According to the EPA, since 1946, this country has been flushing its waste, both toxic and highly radioactive, into the oceans where whales cavort, into the rivers where a few remaining salmon still try to make their way to the ocean, and in streams where trout now gasp for air. According to *National Geographic* magazine, only a shocking nine percent of plastics ever get recycled by companies in the business of recycling.

The result of such an assault on the land, the oceans, as well as on the heavens has been a death sentence, one that was set in place more than a century and a half ago, and which, over that period, has forced a shocking 150 to 200 species of animals and plants into extinction every single day, resulting in what Elizabeth Kolbert, science writer for *The New Yorker*, has called the Sixth Extinction. *The Sixth Extinction: An Unnatural History* is also the title of her book, published in 2014, in which she reports that CO_2 levels increased sharply just about the time of the publication of *Moby Dick,* a period now called the Anthropocene, which places the blame for our cataclysm, not on natural phenomena but on human action. The Grand Extinction began with hunting down whales, followed by drilling for fossil fuel, followed by the levelling of old-growth forests across the country. After which, commercial fisheries began emptying the rivers, streams, and oceans.

The arrogance of such hunting, digging, cutting, and outright slaughter—all for profit—drove the sun and the stars into exile, making the heavens only dimly visible behind the fog of pollutants and poisons, a horror that the guiltiest corporations react to with little or no concern. They should be made to do so, for Kolbert foresees a crisis of staggering proportions: "It is estimated that one-third of all reef-building corals, a third of all freshwater mollusks, a third of sharks and rays, a quarter of all mammals, a fifth of all reptiles, and a sixth of all birds are headed toward oblivion." If trends continue, by century's end, she goes on, "as many as half the earth's species will be gone."

The *Oxford English Dictionary* (OED) defines *extinction* as "the fact or process of becoming extinct; a coming to an end or a dying out; the condition of being extinct." The editors can only present the finality of a species, the cosmic insult of extinction, as mere gerunds—"becoming extinct;" "coming to an end;" "dying out;" "being extinct"—a fading out and a slow dying, but definitely not a finality. The editors of the OED make the idea of extinction resemble a "process," passive and insignificant, and perhaps so natural as to be hardly worth explaining. Or, to be more generous, perhaps in 1933, the year of the dictionary's first edition, the idea sounded so far-fetched that the editors simply could not believe in it. This, even though the Tasmanian Tiger, along with the Heath Hen, went extinct that very year, 1933.

Extinction was real, and even though the Endangered Species Act would be ratified forty years later, the legislation remains powerless against wholesale killing—it is merely a coroner's report. Even its statement of purpose hedges: "The United States has pledged itself as a sovereign state in the international community to conserve to the extent possible all the various species of fish or wildlife and plants facing extinction . . . " Legislation and law not withstanding, all those countless descendants of Ahab, entrepreneurs of the modern age, in their relentless drive to conquer the natural world, have managed to corrupt and pollute not just the Earth and the heavens, along with a good deal of language, but reality, as well. Contemplating the night sky in some open field, campers might look up and wonder: Is that a falling star, a NASA satellite, or some billion-dollar Elon Musk indulgence, its motherboard burned out, drifting back down to Earth? In 2022, the UN estimated that 8,261 satellites orbited the night sky, many of them, at any moment, directly overhead, outnumbering, by far, the 350 North Atlantic right whales and 30 North Pacific right whales that still exist.

In *Moby Dick*, Melville concentrates on Ahab's obsession with hunting down and killing his nemesis, one of the largest beings in creation, Moby Dick. So possessed is Ahab that what he actually sees, in his maniacal vision, is his own transfigurations in that creature "who swam before him as the monomaniac incarnation of all those malicious agencies which some deep men feel eating in them." At the same time, every member of the thirty-person crew, numbed by the routine of continuous killing and blinded by the lure of unlimited money, have signed on to Ahab's version of madness, committing themselves to years of horrific killing and butchering, carried out as if they were merely workers in some factory.

In the middle of the Atlantic, far removed from anyone who could see and judge, even those mightily complicated and miraculous creatures are of little importance to the men aboard the Pequod, for they are concerned with only one thing: not provoking the rage of their unpredictable Captain.

> 'Aye, Starbuck; aye, my hearties all round; it was Moby Dick that dismasted me; Moby Dick that brought me to this dead stump I stand on now. Aye, aye,' he shouted with a terrific, loud, animal sob, like that of a heart-stricken moose; 'Aye, aye! it was that accursed white whale that razed me; made a poor pegging lubber of me for ever and a day!' Then tossing both arms, with measureless imprecations he shouted out: 'Aye, aye! and I'll chase him round Good Hope, and round the Horn, and round the Norway Maelstrom, and round perdition's flames before I give him up. And this is what ye have shipped for, men! to chase that white whale on both sides of land, and over all sides of earth, till he spouts black blood and rolls fin out. What say ye, men, will ye splice hands on it, now? I think ye do look brave.'

Melville shocked his readers by moving them from contemporary renderings of those bucolic adventures of buddies trekking through woods and wildlands, or rafting down fast-moving rivers, or climbing unassailable mountains, to a close accounting of a madman bent on killing whales in the vastness of the ocean. He told it in language that attacks the heart like a coroner's cold account, in details so frightening they dare the reader to continue. *Moby Dick*, then, is the tallest tale turned grotesquely real, at times, laying bare the gory details that encouraged the legally protected, commercial killing of the most majestic, elegant, and mysterious creatures in the natural world.

But Melville did not stop there. He forced his readers to go beyond sanctioned killing, to eavesdrop on the gritty perversions of life aboard ship, describing the prolonged pursuit of the whale, of men entangling it in ropes, of thrusting harpoon after harpoon into its fleshy side, then cutting and slicing until the giant could fight no more, exhausted and bloody, finally giving up its life. In one of Melville's oddest chapters, titled "The Whale as a Dish," we listen to our new-found friend, Ishmael, at a critical point in his eventual revulsion of so much death. Here, he tries to justify the behavior of the ship's second mate, the usually jolly Mister Stubb, who, the night before pestered the Pequod's very old and very tired African cook to roast him a steak from a whale that had been killed that day and was still roped to the boat. Its mighty carcass, a shock to some of the crew, stretched the entire length of the Pequod. The chapter, "Whale as Dish," is number 65, out of a total of 135, almost halfway through the entire telling and thus, appropriately, the proper time to pause for something to eat. Which, in any other circumstance, should be cause for celebration and renewal, in the way meals invite both grace and graciousness.

The chapter opens quite differently, with Ishmael, who has surprisingly turned food connoisseur, in general, and expert on high cuisine and especially on delicacies, describing an ancient delicacy from sixteenth-century France, a dish prepared with the tongue of a Right whale. After retailing the great taste of yet another exotic and gruesome treat, barbequed porpoise, Ishmael then points out that, as any savvy whaler knows, it is in the smallest of the Sperm whales that "the brains are accounted a fine dish," an insipid detail that he glosses over with cooking instructions that make his recipe sound too much like the account of a murder: "The casket of the skull is broken into with an axe, and the two plump, whitish lumps being withdrawn (precisely resembling two white puddings), are then mixed with flour, and cooked into a most delectable mess, in flavor resembling calves' head . . . " The cook then coats the twin lobes with flour, bakes the whale meat in its own oil, after which the crew sits down, without saying Grace, to their helping of whale brains.

It seems clear that Ishmael has tasted the dish himself, perhaps more than once, and in his telling recounts behavior of the forbidden, not of a human being eating the flesh of another human being, but of a mammal eating the flesh of another mammal. And then, that truth seems to hit Ishmael, for while he tries to see a meal of whale brains as no different from eating a steak or a lamb chop, he relies on a rationalization that seems unconvincing: "But no doubt the first man that ever murdered an ox was regarded as a murderer; perhaps he was hung; and if he had been put on his trial by oxen, he certainly would have been; and he certainly deserved it if any murderer does. Go to the meat-market of a Saturday night and see the crowds of live bipeds staring up at the long rows of dead quadrupeds. Does not that sight take a tooth out of the cannibal's jaw? Cannibals? who is not a cannibal? I tell you it will be more tolerable for the Fejee that salted down a lean missionary in his cellar against a coming famine; it will be more tolerable for that provident Fejee, I say, in the day of judgment, than for thee, civilized and enlightened gourmand, who nailest geese to the ground and feastest on their bloated livers in thy paté-de-foie-gras."

We listen to Ishmael at his most disorganized, displaced, and unconvincing struggle to make meaning and to find reason, all of which rings false, for he knows that he has not touched the truth, a trait that does not befit the man whose name translates, "God Hears." Ishmael scrambles to make sense out of what people ingest, out of what they kill in order to survive, of what the crew of the Pequod eats each day. Are there limits? At this halfway point in the voyage, we come up against a crucial moment in the education of that narrator with no name, this Ishmael, who is eager to return to the civilized world and who, in the course of recounting his time aboard the Pequod, becomes more and more orphaned from the gore of that shipboard reality.

There is no skirting the obvious: The chapter describes one mammal eating another mammal—a reprise of Ishmael's great fear about Queequeg, revealed to us in the earliest chapters, as a man with face of "a dark, purplish, yellow color, here and there stuck over with large-blackish looking squares," who sells human heads from New Zealand. What else can he be, Ishmael believes, but a cannibal.

As an indication of how much Ahab has corrupted logic and the natural order, Ishmael, who wanted to put his hatchet to Queequeg for fear he was going to be eaten, here can describe violating one of the most basic taboos in a society without comment from him or a singlemember of the crew. For them, of course, whales could never be considered kin, or even counted as mammals, but must remain the great nuisance of the open seas, not simply unrelated to us, but by their appearance and behavior, so obviously separated and so radically different from human beings. They are a meal, yes, but more importantly, a commodity, a trove of products, an enormous repository of profit. They are creatures, indeed, just begging to be taken apart and sold for their various parts.

Nature, now denatured, has not only lost its invigorating spirit, but also its power to cure. Indeed, like denatured alcohol, it has become poisonous. We must take its suicide note most seriously, broadcast nature's warning, resuscitate those elementals and, once again, come alive ourselves. The contemporary French theorist, Gilles Deleuze, praised Melville for wrenching language out of the ordinary and the usual, mystically rearranging words aimed at upsetting the rational, making us sit up and take notice, to bear down and read, and then reread, as words slip their meaning:

> "Is this not the schizophrenic vocation of American literature: to make the English language, by means of driftings, deviations, de-taxes or sur-taxes (as opposed to the standard syntax), slip in this manner? To introduce a bit of psychosis into English neurosis? To invent a new universality? If need be, other languages will be summoned into English in order to make it echo this divine language of storm and thunder. Melville invents a foreign language that runs beneath English and carries it off: it is the OUTLANDISH or Deterritorialized, the language of the Whale. Whence the interest of studies of *Moby-Dick* that are based on Numbers and Letters, and their cryptic meaning, to set free at least a skeleton of the inhuman or superhuman originary language."

To try to comprehend the notion of "the language of the Whale," one had to scrutinize every word, Melville insisted, as something sacred, a retreat deep into the arcane meanings of the bible, if necessary. Language for Melville found its home in hyperbole, rage, anger, majesty and, of course, beauty, a yearning for the euphoria of the divine made tangible through minute details. But one must be prepared to read in the word the world redefined and renewed. The task is arduous, and it just might require over eight-hundred pages to hear the rustling of leaves as a cry for rain, the flopping of a trout as a cry for air, the bleating of a lamb as a cry for life, the creaking of a tree as a death rattle. Melville translates by slowly slipping the reader into a hypnotic state that moves beyond and behind the rantings of Ahab into the deepest, most mysterious shadings of language. For Deleuze, within the horror that is schizophrenia, meaning takes shape, once again, slowly in the outskirts of outrage.

Choosing language that was so outlandish for traditional fiction but that powered the Manifesto, Melville revealed his strategy, as he began writing *Moby Dick,* in a 1850 note to Hawthorne: "Genius all over the world stands hand in hand, and one shock of recognition runs the whole circle around." "One shock of recognition" fires Melville's own language and empowers every Manifesto, urging readers to re-cognize, to look again and see the horror, hear the truth, and step into the streets.

Melville brought readers frighteningly close to such a colossus that they might get to know the mightiest and most overwhelming whale in its smallest, most minute traits. He was determined to make even the most complacent, agnostic reader understand why biblical narrative favors this mighty being. People do not often see whales—a few catch a glimpse of a tail or a fin on whale-watching excursions, or gawk as a single creature washes ashore, dead, its belly bloated with bits of plastic. It is essential to know that without our bearing witness to their existence, whales persist in miraculous ways. They swim and eat, give birth, nurse, and cavort deep under the sea.

Melville tried to grab hold of a nation that was rapidly transforming into an economic power by situating his tale in the midst of an outsized ocean and with the largest of creatures. How could a country of such huge dimensions, with such oversized personalities and profits, create meaning other than with the tallest Tall Tales turned real? Beauty and majesty, alas, are no mainstays against greed. Over time, this country would bear witness to far too many examples of the most gorgeous, most majestic swaths of nature utterly destroyed, in a most ruthless manner, especially if the trees were ancient and towering, the carp oversized, the moose blessed with enormous antlers, and the bird exotic and able to soar with its wide wingspan. Serial devastation began with the drive to rid the ocean of its most inspiring creatures, moving onto land with drilling for oil and the felling of ancient Redwoods; to the eradication of the earliest tribal peoples on the Plains; on to the extermination of hundreds of thousands of bison; and to the relentless killing of millions of other animals that once flourished in their intricate and sophisticated, remote habitats.

Finally, that lure called progress would reveal itself as something deadly, poisoning the air, the ground, and the watertable with methane, nitrous oxide, carbon dioxide, fluorinated gases and hydrocarbons, heavy metals, and most thoroughly, with micro-plastics that would end their journey (but not their protracted lives) choking the streams, rivers, and oceans, ending up clogging the stomachs of creatures that lived in the water, as well as those on the land.

Revenge and madness have taken hold. On the Pequod's ill-fated voyage, even though he is a well-seasoned, commercial whaler, Ahab has gone beyond killing whales for profit. He has been on such commercial voyages scores of times in the past. For the moment, Ahab's madness has moved beyond the busyness of business. And, thus, Melville marks the icy coldness of the modern world through a perversion of that basic emotion from the ancient world: revenge fueled by outrage. Having perfected his outbursts, Ahab has convinced an entire crew into believing in his disfiguring vision and, what might be worse, into helping and abetting him to achieve his deranged goal: "Command the murderous chalices! Drink ye harpooners! Drink and swear, ye men that man the deathful whaleboat's bow—Death to Moby Dick!" The contemporary literary critic, Helen Vendler, gives that outrageous author his honest due: "Melville is a poet of dangerous social and political observation."

While he is fierce and formidable, casting a long shadow that precedes him, Ahab makes no appearance in the first one-hundred pages. We hear about him, we are made to think and wonder about him, and before we lay eyes on him, we know we ought to fear him. Not until page 103 does that wicked authority finally reveal himself, and then only in the shadows, so that we get but a glimpse of "the elderly man . . . brown and brawny . . . with a fine and almost microscopic network of the minutest wrinkles interlacing round his eyes . . . such eye-wrinkles are very effectual in a scowl." His face frozen as a scowl, Ahab prefers doorways and pasageways, making it near impossible to remark on his presence with any assurance. Only Ishmael, with his ability to see what is barely present, and knowing Ahab at the level of his soul, can catch hold of his "minutest wrinkles."

Ahab has become a monumentally frightening apparition, a larger-than-life projection of someone power-mad and in total command, a toxic side effect of his own deranged, ancient emotion, rage, supercharged here by an infusion of greed. He is a person possessed of an appetite of such staggering proportions that, once primed, his hunger could never be sated; of an anger so intense, his fury could never be tamped down and, most frightening, never extinguished. He has shed all sense of proportion—retreating into a single-minded and singular state, a man without a personality, a captain of a crew who, likewise, has lost all sense of care and compassion. A scoundrel with a scowl, such is the force called Ahab.

The destruction of the natural world now takes place on a scale and at a speed never before imagined, a catastrophe that Melville tried to envision more than one hundred years ago. This is what greed looks like; this is the painful, mundane way the most magnificent of living things end their days, an unleashing of torture by our species that passes without much attention or concern. Melville, the mystic and the prophet, connected the idea of progress with the realities of ruthlessness and killing.

Corporations, especially, flourish by disregarding the plight of animals and nature, of the sacred, and, of course by disregarding all related consequences. People fail to understand how such an attitude came to dominate and then to decimate, and why so few people seem to care that corporate greed has driven scores of sentient creatures into extinction. We must confront that determination to undo creation, to erase existence by eliminating entire species and emptying the Earth of all that lives within it and on it. How can we do anything else?

Today, the ravaging of the Earth for fossil fuel gets carried out by so-called "extraction industries," corporations guilty of poisoning the planet in their lust for oil and all things beyond. It is near impossible to believe the scale of killing that for centuries has continued to destroy almost anything one can imagine. It is difficult, anymore, to be shocked. Numbers do little more than numb. Still, the death toll gets tallied and, still, the animals suffer horrific deaths, resembling nothing we have ever witnessed in our lives. Some creatures, as their habitats and sources of food get snatched from them, suffer for a time and finally give up and die, while others look death in the eye, and see crazed, out of control human behavior, and in that instant—and in that recognition—freeze and remain frozen. For they know only too well death's acrid odor. Others, in an intense desire to survive, flee for their lives. They hide; they shiver in fear. The death of life is manifest and monumental.

Melville demanded a stop to such madness and killing, a movement from knowing into acting. Writing *Moby Dick* took its toll on him. He needed a break from death. His later stories are integral to the Manifesto, showing what it takes to act, or what action means, which he did by creating characters with character. The first, and perhaps most well-known of them is Billy Budd who, upon his immanent hanging aboard ship, sacrificed to quell a mutiny, can only celebrate the person who has condemned him to death, uttering his last words, with a rope hanging about his neck and which is about to be tightened: "God Bless Captain Vere!" The second, like Ishmael, bears a single name, Bartleby, an accountant who responds to whatever is asked of him, even by his own boss, with something assertive, even aggressive, in the form of negation: "I would prefer not to." Hawthorne's thunderclap of a *No* has been toned down and domesticated, but it is still determinedly present.

Herman Melville held a deep commitment to those who courageously held on to the vibrancy of life, to base instinct and principle. In and among the high-pitched chanting and the railing of encroaching madness, one finds in the later Melville a series of curt and cutting, simple sentences, uttered by characters who embody the imperative of the Manifesto: "Call me Ishmael"; "God Bless Captain Vere!"; "I prefer not to," and that most wonderful imperative: "No! in Thunder."

While greed is visible in images of death and audible in cries of pain, it also produces its own, sickeningly acrid odor. In the summer of 2019, thousands of hectares of the Australian Outback burned at extraordinarily high temperatures for months, reducing a huge land mass to ash and to the stench of smoking animal carcasses that were burned alive in their burrows, nests, and native redoubts. These were creatures with the most colorful monikers, like the Mountain Pygmy Possum, the Long-Footed Potoroo, the Yellow-Bellied Glide, the Brush-Tailed Rock Wallaby, along with an array of birds, like the critically threatened Regent Honeyeater. A great many of them have gone forever, names on a rapidly expanding list of extinct species, where that word *extinct* slowly loses both its meaning and its sting.

Ethnologists estimated more than one billion such fiery deaths in the Outback. In their desperate urge to escape the flames, those creatures met their deaths head-on, thrashing and writhing in agony; dying of the most unnatural causes; dying while trying to reach the edge of their world and salvation, their powerful instinct to survive propelling them straight to the sea. No matter if we classify or define finely and forever, no matter if we calculate precisely with numbers or suggest mysteriously with metaphors, the reality persists—an unimaginable array of animals, on this planet, no longer sing, or swim, run, hop or fly.

We all might have taken action earlier if we had seen more clearly and more closely, which is to say, if we had looked upon the natural world with a sense of wonder and delight, but which is impossible when the Earth has for so long been a mere resource; when screen after screen insists on our attention; on which devastation has been transformed into an art project; when memory is measured in bytes, and love in award-winning Netflix episodes.

Ahab's voyage reveals the catastrophic result of greed coupled with the insatiable hunger of an overweening ego. At the end of its aborted voyage, the Pequod and every person aboard has perished, except for one character-elect, as we know all too well, the one in need of a name. He is narrator-in-chief, but a modified version, for he is not interested in creating a convincing story but, rather, in talking off the top of his head and from memory, doing little more than free-associating and recounting events as fast and as accurately as he can remember them. If there is something beyond a mere stream, called an "ocean of consciousness," Ishmael possesses it.

In the first chapter of *Moby Dick*, titled "Loomings," Melville introduces Ishmael along with a history that looms over him, a history that has dogged him his entire life. Ishmael seems to take his place behind an imaginary loom weaving his old-fashioned narrative, like some trickster spider, or one of the three solemn Moirai, who weave the pattern of a person's life, sounding off for anyone who will listen, in a fate fast-looming, in which any one of those three sisters just might decide it is time, and cut his thread.

Ishmael must be stingy with his telling—neither flamboyant nor colorful—because with every word he risks his life, and thus his being is a most remarkable and generous gift to us. Ishmael cannot revise, for he is thinking out loud, speaking in the moment. He is recalling, recollecting, remembering, and perhaps even embellishing, as he steers clear of the lie.

Sailors use the term *looming* to refer to the outline of an object as it gradually comes into view, emerging out of a fog and hovering slightly above the surface of the water. *Moby Dick* opens with a title suggesting that, through the fog of remembering, as we set sail in the easy gale of its telling, the story will slowly emerge, slowly dawning on us.

Neck deep in water, a parody of Christian naming by immersion and a distorted amniotic (re)birth, Ishmael, if we fantasize freely, has been baptized, converted, undergoing the longest confession imaginable—delivered to us in an ordination of intimacy that bars us from making judgments. We have been denied the privilege of questioning or doubting: We listen and we receive and, simply by being, we provide comfort.

As we begin reading and listening to an adventure that persists beyond the limits of human endurance, we grow uncertain of the fate of the person in charge of the telling, an outsider who charts our course. Just how long, we are made to wonder, can this one person go on speaking; and, indeed, we might even ask, what drives him to go on speaking? Why does he care so much that he would risk his life for the sake of telling a tale? The scene is a fairy tale, a sci-fi wonder, a sea-shanty chanted to the heavens. Ishmael has sinned against Nature. Ishmael has repented.

More to the point, why should such a bizarre recounting of death and destruction be preserved? Scores of whaling ships have been shattered and sunk. What is so interesting about this one? Shouldn't Ishmael be saving himself, trying to stay alive as long as possible with tiny breaths of air? Shouldn't he be more concerned with signaling some rescue vessel? Doesn't this seemingly long-winded fellow need every gulp of air, small or large? Is this tale so important that he must deliver it to a total stranger, and to one who has no way of rescuing that poor soul?

We do not know if he will be there until the end of the telling—the reader constantly frightened that Ishmael is so close to going under and that, unlike the whale, he will run out of air and luck and will not re-emerge from the depths of the ocean. He has already told us, in the very first chapter, that he can so easily "grow hazy about the eyes, and begin to be over-conscious of my lungs." All that now looms over his life, in his eyes, mouth, and lungs, does not look promising. Unwinding his narration, Ishmael inches closer and closer to his watery demise, as if, in some monumental sacrifice, he is giving up his life just for us—a true sacrifice, one might suppose, in the domain of the storyteller, who is alive solely because of the buoyancy of words.

In this passion play of life and death, starring an enormous, translucent whale, Melville turns the act of reading, neither simply nor only, into some religious practice—Ishmael as confessor; reader as priest—but into a moral excursion, as well. We are being coached in the act of caring. The longer we commit to listening, the longer we keep this lone survivor, a stranger named Ishmael—unknown and yet known—afloat in the water, bobbing and babbling, safe from drowning. We ought to be reading slowly and with compassion, for his words are charged with meaning. As narrator, he forces us into the profound experience of hearing as acting, reading as caring, killing as commerce, almighty objection as Manifesto.

But the more time we spend hearing and pondering, the more we become culpable in both Ishmael's suffering and his survival. We ought to race to the Epilogue as fast as possible. How insidious of Melville, to make the act of reading an anxious and guilty one, while we seem to be moored in the middle of oceanica. He has scrambled the logic of reading and narration by tying the reader so radically to the telling. What should we do? Must we speed read to reach the end? Can this prose even be read fast? In this book, reading carries ethical implications.

Moby Dick can be read as Ishmael's last will and testament, as well as his memoir, the two loomed together. More than that, the recounting of Ahab and his nemesis Moby Dick provides the grist for Melville's own Manifesto, an argument and a demand that unfolds through Ishmael. It is Ishmael's take on Ahab that we must believe; it is his belief in redemption that we must embrace; it is his repulsion of killing that must give us hope. And through it all, we know Ishmael to be someone who speaks the truth. After all, what does he have to lose? Ishmael's telling resembles a final will and testament, a time when the only thing that might save him keeps us interested in the truth, in hearing and overhearing. Or, he just might feel, why not tell the truth, for my end is upon me?

Melville tempts us to marvel at Ishmael's final moments in which he is willing to spend his remaining few breaths on us, his invisible ear. We can agree; we can call him Ishmael, even though he cannot reciprocate: He cannot call us anything. He goes under water for a bit, comes up, and his sometimes-slurred rant turns slowly and methodically, sentence by sentence, into an extended tale of pain, anguish, misery, and, of course, killing. In his stammering sincerity, we must find hope—for there is so much that needs to be changed.

Melville's injunction is mighty, huge, and distended—perhaps even impossible. Every suggestion and solution to the devastation of the Earth must be oversized, fueled by the intensity of Ahab's rage and the distortions of Melville's prose, from Ishmael's demands on us, to Moby Dick's percussive power against the Pequod, from the length of the book to the overwhelming injunction to halt killing now. In our catastrophic epoch, we cannot back away from the impossible, for the end is closing in fast. To cap global warming at that 1.5 degrees C. over pre-industrial times, we must reduce greenhouse gas emissions 45 percent by 2030 and reach net zero by 2050.

Because life on Earth is under threat of extinction, we must radically reinterpret our spirit and destiny. Intent on stopping eco-murder, Melville Shanghaied the reader out to sea—a practice popular in the 1850s—to a new horizon and perspective, to witness the killing of the mighty and the majestic. Melville reveals his revulsion by situating the name of the whaler, the Pequod, within one of the country's most shameless acts of killing. The Pequot people lived on territory that would become Connecticut. In 1636, a coalition of colonists who needed more land for their crops attacked the Pequot village, burning down their homes and killing over 700 people.

The Pequod departed Nantucket on Christmas Day, turning its back on the birth of Christ in favor of the death of whales, and listing dangerously from its heavy cargo of hatred and rage. When the Pequod sinks, so does an era and an attitude, providing Melville the chance to revitalize language and literature. Dispensing with the familiar in storytelling, along with acceptable sentence structure, grammar, and at times, logic, Melville abandoned style, making both the power of the Manifesto and the wonder of the natural world to come fully alive.

Melville underscored his experiment, perhaps in homage to those sonic wonders, the whales, with a literary trope called Voice. Whereas style can be conscripted from any period and imposed on prose, voice takes its life from reactions in the moment. For style to be effective, some crisis must prompt people to speak out loud. Something shockingly elusive, and even frightening forces that shout into being. Voice makes people brazen, prompting both immediacy and intimacy, resonance in a single word that describes speaking and writing, lungs and language: volume. Voice makes itself most apparent in our first cry for life, our tiny crowning or breaching, akin to some water-based mammal, forgoing the amniotic bath for fresh air, announcing our arrival: I am here, a power as yet uncontained. Take heed and, quick, call me something.

And because Voice, above all else, relies on breath and breathing—sentences, too, must come up for air—vowels over consonants, assonance over alliteration, pitch over persuasion, the elegiac over the meditative. Such an emphasis on breath, oddly enough, favors consonantal languages, like Phoenician, Hebrew, and Arabic, as opposed to, say, Italian, Portuguese, Spanish, French, or even English. Consonantal languages can only be read aloud, breath a living substitute for vowels—*vowel* and its variants, *vow* and *avowal*, *provoke* and *invoke*, share a root in *voice*—and, like God breathing into clay and bringing Adam to life, the speaker's breath animates the consonants, bringing inert characters to life as words, and then bringing words to life as characters.

Voice is the *Shʾma* of literature, the idea that, to understand, one must push beyond the sometimes-listless act of listening, to the intensity of hearing. Voice is a lure, or maybe merely alluring, with its promise of intimacy. As we set sail, propelled by its booming shouts and epithets of hate, unsettling prose rhythms, and more, *Moby Dick* seems freighted with voice and perhaps even overwhelmed by it: Everyone and everything speaks, from the waves to the terns, from the whales to the wind, and even to the listless creaking of the Pequod's keel: The world is alive. We have sailed into the past, into a time when nature spoke.

From every direction, there comes noise and notes of discord—gulls screeching in maddening circles, whales blowing air and water, and a crew shouting demands that negate prior demands. The water-logged vessel moves at the will of the wind; each greenhand demanding a witness; nobody and nothing there does not yearn to be heard. Killing aboard a whaler is deafening and chaotic, a messy and clumsy spree of killing, a victory over life, sounded in huzzas of horror, in days freed from the usual twelve-hours of wakefulness.

We meet the sentences of that New England brooder at the depth of full-fathom five, those grave lines of Herman Melville, in his unmuzzled state—far from any trace of Boston Brahmin aloofness—breaking the bonds and boundaries of literature. As albino, even the whale betrays logic. On deck of the Pequod, there are a parade of people of different colors and countries—thirty or more crewmembers building their own towering babble.

Voice is much more than mere speaking. Voice is the expression of Melville, not just as an author with the volume turned up, but as an authority pitched to the whale's ear with a warning; and here, voice is Melville at his most direct. To hear him requires more than listening, something closer to sacred hearing from the bible—again, the Sh'ma of understanding. We must pay strict attention, learning anew how to comprehend the word, for Melville is in charge certainly as author, but much more as authority and seer.

And so, voice is Herman Melville's way of declaiming what he knows, an outspoken loudmouth waking and warning his readers; and voice is Herman Melville, as a character staring directly back at us, whose truth echoes with manifest immediacy. Finally, with a voice pitched so high and so loud, Melville's words linger and hover, making certain we read him correctly. Herman Melville has crafted his own language of knowing: A voice of insistence in the might of the Manifesto.

The Industrial Revolution was looming, and people felt the change of rhythm in their daily lives, in their stride, in their speaking, and the rapidity with which they made their choices and their purchases, transactions suddenly stripped bare of barter and banter, and eventually of money, itself—demanding a different way of seeing and thus knowing, a new rhythm of breathing, and a new vocabulary able to capture those new and radical dislocations.

People needed to be informed of change in so-called real time, which meant stripping events of their complexities and subtleties of interpretation. The ticker tape, new in the 1860s, allowed stock brokers to transact in real time—profit in an instant. A grand robbery was taking place, and the precious object, stolen in plain view, was nothing less than reality, itself. Once the old pace of life had been supplanted, it would prove impossible to retrieve it, for dynamos grew more powerful, revolved more rapidly and more loudly—with few or nobody wanting them to slow down. People took comfort in the new power and its purported dependability. By 1851, the word *horse-power* had lost its hyphen and its animal connections, so that the catalog for the Great Exhibition could refer to "an oscillating steam-engine of ten horsepower." And people knew it meant something other, something more than ten horses pulling a wagon. Horsepower meant engine capacity, measured in cubic inches, power made audible in a new measurement called revolutions-per-minute, or RPMs.

The wreckage of the Pequod symbolizes the end of a world but also the beginning of a new and protracted time, one that dismantled and destroyed the familiar— an incredibly brittle period, in which trust got replaced by the new-fangled promise to revolutionize people's lives into something remarkable through the mechanization of the everyday.

This was true—as incredible as it sounds—even of language, which towards the end of the nineteenth century developed new words, like *train, revolver, pulley, telegraph, camera*, and new psychological terms, like *agoraphobia*, along with the repulsive *Negrophobia* and, in 1856, a near epidemic of fear and nervousness labelled *neurasthenia*. Reacting to the proliferation of the neologism, and to the many changes in meaning of old ones, in 1857, board members of the Philological Society of London called for a new dictionary. Close to thirty years later, in 1884, lexicographers produced the first fascicle of the *Oxford English Dictionary*.

Herman Melville disrupted our entrance into the corrupting, highly industrialized, thoroughly mechanized, and consumptive age, and made us pay attention: Smack in front of us lingered the wreck of our ship of state, the

tale of ruin told by someone near drowning, bobbing hap-
lessly in the vastness of the Atlantic. Something has gone
terribly wrong, beyond the odd and amusing. In the new
industrial age, people had become orphaned, displaced, in
need of being called a name and in need of a calling. They
were certainly in need of knowing, for even narration
turned out to be unreliable, shedding rational, reliable
telling for a drowning sailor in Melville, an illiterate ado-
lescent in Twain, a madman in Poe, a Transparent Eyeball
in Emerson, a so-called idiot in Faulkner, and "the most
terrific liar you ever saw," Holden Caulfield. The word
abnormal entered the language in 1835, appearing first in
Richard Hoblyn's *Dictionary of Medical Terms.*

Only a few years after the swamping of the Pequod,
harpoons continued to pierce deep into the flesh of
whales, but in the new machine age, human effort was
replaced by cannons mounted on the bow of the ship's
deck. Powered by black powder, and fitted with scopes,
men fired harpoons with uncanny accuracy, over great
distances, each round a guaranteed kill, for as the harpoon pierced the whale's flesh, a grenade exploded—
instantaneous death.

Leave the deck of the Pequod, enter the town and look
around: Handiwork of every kind was being scrapped to
make way for some new, alluring machine that carried
out routine work much more quickly, accurately, efficiently, and most importantly, more cheaply and without
complaint.

Wherever people seemed to wander in that accelerated world, they came up against something new, startling, and mechanized: the sewing machine, the telephone, the trolley, the camera, the typewriter, the train, the escalator, the elevator, the safety bicycle, the time clock, the revolver, and the Gatling gun. One might even spot a helicopter or an airship crossing the sky.

Not only were people encountering new machines almost everywhere they turned, but with the introduction of the automobile, they actually sat on or in a machine and assumed the controls themselves, becoming truly auto-mobile. By 1890, an oddity appeared at key intersections, called the stop sign, which instructed drivers to halt their machines for those outmoded pedestrians. On May 12, 1901, Connecticut placed a limit on speed, the first in the country—ten miles-per-hour on city streets, and twelve on country roads. Just after the turn of the century, in 1901, Ransom Eli Olds, the son of a blacksmith, introduced his stylish creation, the Oldsmobile.

By design, *Moby Dick* cannot be read in a single sitting. To be effective, a Manifesto must both agitate and arrest readers, slowing them down more and more until they come to a full stop. Melville's critique of impending horror must be read as a document of extreme urgency and insistence, a demand to protect all of creation and to pause, think, and then to act. Its title has been ceded, not to a person, but to a mammal, a whale that should not be named. The Manifesto must present reality in such stark terms that its demand for a change in attitude, and then in policy, seems not only reasonable but inevitable. First must come that critical change in people's own attitudes and then in their own vision.

Literature could no longer disregard the state of the natural world, but it needed a new form. By shedding the traditional outlines of the novel, Melville reached a level of critical independence that was most effectively delivered in a statement of revolutionary intent and will. Melville revealed how gratuitous killing could result in the total erasure of the natural world. He insisted that we listen; he demanded that we pay attention. He cast his eye on society and refused to shed a tear, to acquiesce, or to turn away, for he was, himself, far too outraged, far too much in the know about the consequences of a population under the sway of some unhinged, power-hungry dictator, who he hoisted up the main mast for us to see in all his bellowing and bluster. No one who cares about sanity can suffer a distortion like Ahab. No one who cares about sentient life can tolerate such a madman, his unpredictable eccentricity, or his explosive, destructive willpower.

For Melville, conciliation and compromise are simply not acceptable. As he moved farther and farther away from the expectations of the novel, he sailed off into the uncharted territory of seared and, at times, scorched emotions, under the sometimes-terrifying demands of a version of capitalism rushing full-speed into the unknown, the uncharted. Singularly possessed, he ignored harsh reviews and dismal sales.

Moby Dick does not so much require reading as it demands tolerance—for the way it disorients readers and provokes them into reflecting. *Moby Dick* does not require readers as much as it demands thinkers and activists, those who can hear and overhear with a certain clarity. Which is to say, it aims for a slowed-down, contemplative rumination on the sorry state of nature, the crooked hearts that took it down, and an extrapolation into what might pass for a future.

For Melville, in its full-blown, nineteenth-century iteration, the novel had been exhausted. The drawing room, the board room, the bedroom, commanded interest no longer. Now, it was the natural world and our callous treatment of it that called for serious attention. Even *Walden*, a meditation on the glories of nature, written but a mile from Concord, was too much of a retreat from the realities of a ravished Earth.

The new regime, fascinated by mechanical speed, efficiency, and power, chose industrialization over ethics and the protection of the natural world. Melville knew it would be impossible for people to back off from such undoing of the rational: "There is no folly of the beast of the earth that is not infinitely outdone by the madness of men." Such a magnified tale of terror and madness could only be told on that grand Oceanica, on a voyage, up close and in the heart of chaos, madness, and killing, far out of range of eye and ear, beyond the horizon of noticing, in a place without borders or measure—the expanse of the sea—in a ship that may seem calm, but aboard which holds a crew who comes dangerously, dispassionately alive through killing, which comes to port as commerce and cosmetics.

On the ocean, everything normal turns odd and amplified. One remains, continuously, in the middle of its vastness, inside its weather, shouting to be heard, gesticulating to be seen, taking risks just to be acknowledged as a living being. Life gets enlarged and distorted into a caricature of the real and the actual. In the rush to kill, in the rendering of flesh, and in the cult of cash, life gets diminished—for both the killed and the killer. Men rearrange the idea of life by removing the largest, most noble of its creatures. Whales are determined to stay alive; whalers are determined to snuff out their lives.

In the end, Herman Melville left the library for the lectern. What will he deliver, one wonders—perhaps a sermon? More pointedly, Herman Melville will deliver his warning to every last person, in Manifestos of deep concern, of lofty indignation, underscored by a thunderous NO. He insisted that we do more than hear his word and that, in the most highly charged sense, we overhear. In the newly invigorated and recalibrated world, one inspirited by people trying to hang on to their own sense of being against the rapid takeover by dynamos, dynamite, and derricks, it falls not on the politician, and certainly not on the scientist/engineer to act as the people's seer and the Earth's savior: It is the artist who sees most clearly.

We will come to our senses only through the insistence of someone like Herman Melville, who takes us back to an earlier time and makes us witnesses to the wonder of everything that is, just as it is. How much mightier, more powerful, and courageous can a creature become than a whale, who will eventually best his foe, survive harpoon wounds, escape yards of encircling, thick ropes, and defeat its killers.

The converted, contrite, and half-dead Ishmael, who has been wronged, wrung out, and finished by the interminable lust for killing and commerce, comes closer to acting as our guide, to narrating our own condition, than anyone even remotely resembling Ahab, blinded, crippled, and deranged as he is, and no longer by rage but, finally, by his misplaced hatred. For Ishmael, the telling of his tale must make him feel that nothing matters much but salt and water, and beyond that, only more salt and much more water. Not even on shaky ground, Ishmael rests on something far less substantial, and yet he is handing us Melville's will and testament for the Earth, his Manifesto delivered to so-called survivors, while spinning his yarn—in the lingo of the sea, looming it—far from shore. For Melville, the deepest of seas may be the right place for his narrator, for as he put it: "Yes, as everyone knows, meditation and water are wedded together."

In the history of Manifestos, one of the most well-known is the *Communist Manifesto*, which, in its spare twenty-three pages demands freedom for every worker in the world. It set a powerful standard, most obviously, in its political intent. The *Manifesto*, written in German, was first published in 1848, and not in English until 1888. If Melville had known of its existence, he might have been enticed to extend its demands to include the liberation of all of nature. The opening line of the *Communist Manifesto* borders on the eerie: "A spectre is haunting Europe—the spectre of Communism." Its final sentence, just as well-known, has become a near cliché of political awakening: "Workers of the world, unite!"

Written in three sections, including a preamble and a conclusion, and demanding open revolt, the *Communist Manifesto* begins with ghosts, as white and transparent as Moby Dick, and concludes with flesh; it opens with creatures hiding and closes with people demanding to be seen and heard. It first describes what it wants and ends with a call for what it needs—namely, nothing less than for the oppressed to grab hold of their freedom because, to quote from a line on Marx's tombstone, "You have nothing to lose but your chains."

To be effective, any Manifesto must offer a view of the world that is greater and more emphatic, much more convincing than what passes for the usual criticism. It must insist on an individual giving up the personal *I,* for the chance to join the much more powerful, satisfying, liberating *We.* A person must first become an individual, free and independent, before he or she can risk entering, "We the people."

The *Communist Manifesto* is emphatic in its serious social or political critique, namely, the liberation of the individual, the freeing of the mind, followed by the near electrical awakening of a person's inner spirit. All of which must culminate in collective action, a march toward unity and the strike for nothing less than—equivocation be gone—total, thorough, and immediate equity, the imperative of change against everything and anything that oppresses. While no one would call Melville a political revolutionary, he did highlight the fast-approaching and highly corrosive expansion of capitalism, through its violent extractions of oil. He warned of the maniacal drive of entrepreneurs for more and more money, while those who labored got as little as possible.

To bring the news about such an epidemic of greed in the country—to break such a powerful grip on the soul of the nation—demanded that Melville shift from the expectations of the nineteenth-century novel to another, more radical way of impressing the most shocking truth on readers. Melville demanded something enormous, namely changing the nature of human nature by alerting readers to the Earth under duress. For such urgency,

Melville needed a form that disturbed and dislodged. He chose the Manifesto.

Melville is not interested in personal liberation, and more in the amalgam of the races—the Pequod boasts a radical entanglement of races and ethnicities. But first and foremost, Melville demands a freeing of nature from the violent excesses of human behavior. The salvation of nature rests on sane human nature. The warning flashes again and again: The wilderness retreating, animal habitats disappearing, nature losing species. The titans of industry were hell-bent on grabbing everything in sight on the Earth, and everything out of sight under it—every single thing that might be sold.

Every leaf, flower, nut, and kernel of life was fodder for commerce, ripe for commodification, ready for sale. The masters of the machinic made their intentions clear, on changing the contours and outlines of the Earth, on leveling, scraping, dynamiting, blasting, hydraulically fracturing and, in general, destroying nature. All creatures suffered. The WWF reports that since 1970 humans have killed a grotesque seventy percent of all wildlife.

A Manifesto can only assume a somewhat uncomfortable, shocking, surprising, and above all, revolutionary point of view, tone, and temper, either quite explicitly or metaphorically. It must startle, making stupefied readers aware that it is possible for them to come alive and embrace life anew. Such documents are usually composed in the throes of some political uprising, demanding radical change, promising a renewed life of freedom, a reward for its own sake. The Manifesto does more: It demands decisive action and a radical shift in the conduct of people's lives.

The Manifesto underscores liberation, not just with its argument, but in its radical rearrangement of word order and syntax, driven by the peculiar pitch of the author's voice and political insistence, and thus a great many Manifestos emerge from radical artistic movements—the Futurists, Dadaists, Acmeists, Surrealists, Situationists, and, most notably, the Italian Futurists, with its feisty leader, Filippo Tommaso Marinetti, who, on February 20, 1909, released *The Manifesto of Futurism.* With one hand clutching his pen, and the other clenched into a fist, raised high in the air, Marinetti sent a wish list as ultimatum into the world: "1. We want to sing about the love of danger, about the use of energy and recklessness as common, daily practice. 2. Courage, boldness and rebellion will be essential elements in our poetry. 3. Up to now, literature has extolled a contemplative stillness, rapture, and reverie. We intend to glorify aggressive action, a restive wakefulness, life at the double, the slap and the punching fist." In his recharged and re-imagined reality, Marinetti traded dynamite for firecrackers, screaming for speaking, action for lassitude.

The thorough-going power and insistence of the Futurist Manifesto prepared the way for the Surrealist

Manifesto, concocted by the French writer, poet, and founder of the aesthetic movement, Andre Breton, in October 1924, and written in praise of "beloved imagination, what I most like in you is your unsparing quality." For Breton, ordinary thinking and reactions induce self-delusion. Revolution demands a pair of lungs for yelling, eyes for envisioning, and feet for marching those ideas across town and impressing them into the consciousness of the people. Breton called for an inspirited madness, beyond the kind of "madness that locks one up," to that sort of the carefully deranged that one senses in Melville, sounding loud and louder, to be heard over the din of modernity.

Moby Dick comes out of an America that, in the middle of the nineteenth century, had cleaved apart in fairly short order: The first West Africans were dragooned to Virginia in 1619. Their overlords, the so-called Puritans, did not arrive until some ten years later, in 1630, convincing their God of the inferiority of those they needed to enslave. The Constitution was not ratified until 1790. A scant sixty years later, *Moby Dick* was published. Ten years later, in 1861, this nation cleaved in two. 620,000 people would die on the battlefield, five times that number from disease.

Perhaps such a gross indifference was solid preparation, for this country would soon become a nation of justifications, in need of explaining away slavery and genocide, prejudice and hatred, corporate greed and pollution, the decimation of the animal and plant populations, and finally the immanent death of the planet. *Moby Dick* appeared just when America was entering, if not a new century, then a new time, a moral, ethical, and religious moment of deep reckoning, which the nation has still not fully faced and from which it still struggles to recover. It entered a new era and mode, marked by speed, personal power, and racial hatred, ideas and issues moving far too fast for reconciliation.

On August 28, 1830, Peter Cooper's steam-powered locomotive, the Tom Thumb, made its initial run on newly laid tracks, reaching a top speed of 13 mph. By 1854, trains were traveling at an astonishing 60 mph. This country was fast divesting itself of its old raiment, its old way of being, and preparing for a dress-rehearsal in the new and raucous cotillion called Modernity. Over forty years after its premiere in London, the World's Columbia Exposition opened in Chicago in 1893. Newspapers proclaimed the new machines "the incarnation of American power and technology."

The new world, not of wonder but of might, under the control of the "science class," had not simply arrived. It had taken immediate charge. The new internal-combustion machinery of production, primed to operate well beyond "full steam ahead," demanded fuel and oil to keep its engines "revving" at full speed.

Machines disrupted logic and upset expectations. In 1755, Samuel Johnson had declined to include the word *civilization* in his dictionary, deeming it too uncertain a term. It appeared for the first time, and in a perfunctory sense only, in 1775, in Reverend John Ash's dictionary. The editors of the *Oxford English Dictionary*, in 1933, could not find an instance of the word, *civilization,* in its modern sense, until twenty-eight years after the publication of *Moby Dick*, not until the year 1879. The *Dictionary of American Regional English* records the use of the words *civil, civilize,* and *civility*, but, as of 1864, not a single citation for *civilization*. That concept, as shocking as it might seem, apparently did not figure in political discussions in this country. Remember, in 1885, Huck can complain that the Widow Douglas wants to "sivilize" him, which means reading to him from the bible and teaching him spelling.

In the America of 1851, then, that most basic concept, civilization, was still something very much not agreed upon—if it ever could be. Mark Twain was still having fun with it. We may have moved directly from Melville's mid-nineteenth-century America, into the age of the machine, and pell-mell into an undefined future of artificiality, driven by the demands of capitalism, stalling in the twenty-first century when the environment revolted in earnest, smashing headlong into our expectations of a panoply of never-ending resources. In 1851, when Ishmael began yapping, neck-deep in water and surrounded by bits of the Pequod—not a convincing picture of the coming age of machines—the idea of civilization had but a ghostly presence.

In that absence, Melville is not simply writing. He is taking us back to a much earlier and different time, when the natural world was infused with myth, animated by spirits from the four elements, when saying the name of a creature, Livyatan, laid bare its essence. By 1818, Frankenstein's monster, standing outside a French schoolroom, could already boast that he had "learned the science of letters." The bit of language he knows, he got by memorizing a set of rules. In such a desacralized time, Ishmael can find a mythos only in the bible, and in response to his opening line, he forces us into playing the role of Adam, naming the narrator and thus revealing his essence.

This is a bold move, for in 1851, naming does not reveal the essence of anything, but merely indicates possession. Ahab must name the nasty, irritable bull Sperm whale, because he has to bring that wonder to life as a singular creature, identifiable not solely by its appearance, but by its behavior, as well. It carries the name, Moby Dick, so that it can be killed. Melville writes knowing there is no definition yet of civilization, giving him the freedom to reveal the free and full wonder of nature itself. When people aim to end life at its most majestic, or enslave its people, or kill each other on the battlefield, civilization must remain nameless or inchoate. Melville is thus issuing a warning because a Manifesto sends up a flare, illuminating itself and its underbelly. Melville puts his readers and listeners on full alert.

What we witness in *Moby Dick*, then, is something far short of a civilizing moment, or of civility, itself. Instead, Melville attempts to capture sensibility, as it teeters at the brink and, one feels, threatens to spill over into chaos. Civil order is but a whisper short of mutiny, conspiracy but a breath short of complacency. Whales, and all huge creatures in general, will be replaced in their realm of wonder, by horrendously large and aggressive, earth-moving machinery, in the realm of the new corporate reality, with suggestive monikers like Big Brutus, a steam-shovel sixteen stories tall, able to fill three railroad cars with a single scoop, or Big Bertha, Big Muskie, and the mightiest of all mining machines, weighing 13,500 tons, the Bagger. The Earth might survive the stab of a shovel, but will certainly perish under the assault of an army of gargantuan steam-shovels.

What could the voyage of the Pequod mean for Melville's convoluted idea of the American novel, for the corralling of the American mind? Is the entire enterprise of freedom and democracy built, so to speak, on nothing more substantial than the vastness, depth, and instability of water, along with a collection of ethnicities, under the command of a madman, ever eager to pounce, kill, and profit from destroying life and meaning with repeated lunges of a sharpened lance? If true, if, indeed, violence rules, then the entire enterprise known as America exists as a frightening and mean-spirited force, bent on destroying itself. And the nation had not yet entered that most uncivil cleaving, the Civil War.

In his descriptions of minute-by-minute life aboard the Pequod, in the middle of the vast ocean, on a vessel with no easy exit, Melville offered readers a close-up-look at what a so-called civilized, cheek-to-jowl, shoulder-to-shoulder life, one lacking real intimacy, might look like. Here was life rigidly organized, secured by rules, orders, and commands, held in check by an obvious and immoveable power structure, punishments meted out with force and expedience, without regret or remorse and certainly without much sense of justice. It is life with its contents laid bare, peopled with slaves, who managed to escape their dreadful fates, not much different from what life looked like on land and especially in a high-minded, caste-conscious, Brahmin society. Here was life, aboard ship, with all facades gone—a rough and rugged version of civilization afloat, but here with a mixture of colors and hues, of religions and nationalities, seeming to co-exist.

Melville is writing that significant omission of the word *civilization* into some kind of reality—before it is seized upon by a cadre of money-loving Ahabs. And when that concept takes hold and the definition appears, in the next century, it will explode with a force, neither from intellect nor from reason, and certainly not from some radical ideas. It will come only from a fancily constructed and exclusive idea of civilization, fueled by mass production, exploitation, and commerce, notable now for its eerie silence of clerks carrying out transactions electronically, on the fifteenth floor of some high rise, windows sealed, where, tucked inside their carrels and cubicles, scores of Bartlebys who would "prefer not to," resist, feebly, with an "ok" or a "sure." They respond with "all right," when nothing for them is right.

In 1851, Melville knew only too well that such a young nation teetered on an edge such that, at any moment, America's most naïve notion of itself, as a grand and inclusive democracy, or in the language of its founding documents, a Republic, might collapse into a grotesque and distended nation of exploitation and monumental desecration of the very land on which people had staked their tents. And entrepreneurs did just that, marking the Earth with deep scar tissue in a mere forty years after *Moby Dick*, amassing fortunes out of what Faulkner called "that unstoried wilderness."

The greedy ones did not disappoint, pushing the rest of the population, full speed, into a most conspicuous and disfiguring disaster, so that they no longer knew how to act, or worse, how to extract themselves from a catastrophe of their own making. People began to feel desperate, struggling to get by, stumbling and falling, sending the opioid/fentanyl addictions ever higher, while young people descended into depressions ever deeper. Rage finds its expression in a most lethal weapon, the AR-15, which, when modified can fire an astonishing 400 rounds per minute, close to seven bullets a second:

The first twenty weeks of 2021 saw over two hundred mass shootings, in churches and synagogues, in supermarkets and high schools, ending with the most ferocious year on record—692 gruesome events. According to the Gun Violence Archive, 2022 came in second, with 648 mass shootings. In the first 24 days of 2023, 69 people were killed in 39 mass shootings. "(A mass shooting means more than four people, excluding the shooter, died within twenty-four hours of the event.) By mid-November, that number had reached 602, on pace to reach 700 by year-end. Since 2018, according to the *New York Times*, six of the nine deadliest mass shootings in the United States have been carried out by shooters who were twenty years of age or younger. More and more elementary and high school teachers see their profession as dangerous, and enter the classroom with books and a Glock. The country is at war with its own madness.

In this well-established, highly civilized but utterly deadening life, especially one that seems on the edge of total collapse, people do not know what life can even look like. Many cannot muster enough strength to keep going. Scientists issue warnings, but their solutions typically turn counterproductive. High school students suffer from climate despair, adults from something new called "death of despair." Some young people organize, confronting their elders with the truth, a few even suing the government for denying them their future. Far too many of them take their own lives. We have been abandoned to ourselves, orphans shipwrecked, up to our neck in hot water, waiting to be rescued. The rub, of course, is that we can only rescue ourselves. If we could take that news to heart, so many animals would rejoice.

Just one hundred corporations world-wide, all of them in the business of producing fossil fuels, are responsible for seventy percent of the greenhouse gases, killing the planet, wiping out a staggering number of animals, as if they were political radicals, deliberately in the way, intent on blocking this nation's goal of hurling somewhere, far into the future, at top speed. This country has traded the problems of the farm for the horrors of factory-farmed animals, engineered fish, and genetically modified produce. Pigs must be injected with antibiotics to prevent pneumonia; cows stand two feet deep in their own excrement; turkeys, breast heavy and off-balance, can barely walk, let alone fly. We have sprayed almost every inch of the country with poison, a good deal of it delivered from airplanes, deadly particulates contaminating everything . . . everywhere, lingering in the air, the ground, and the groundwater, for long stretches of time.

The largest meat producer in the world, JBS, a Brazilian Company with factories in the US, Australia, Canada, Europe, Mexico, New Zealand, and the UK, "processes," as the company calls its torture and slaughter, 50,000 cows a week in each of its nine facilities in the U.S., along with 80,000 hogs, and 20,000 chickens, as well what the website refers to as "incidental fowl." In

2021, JBS produced 421.6 million metric tons of CO2, more than Italy for an entire year.

Such are the gross numbers of only one conglomerate. The pork chop on a dinner plate is the product of torture, pharmaceuticals, and cruelty. Not just pigs, but all factory-produced animals must be injected with antibiotics to keep them alive long enough to "process" them and get their fancy cuts and tasty parts to market, before some disease infects the meat, forcing the company into the financial loss of a "recall." Cows can live up to twenty years. On farms, they might reach six; on factory farms, only around four. Milk cows must undergo the horror of a medieval torture device, keeping them constantly pregnant through artificial insemination; dairy workers call it "the rape rack."

The antibiotics that people consume in their Big Macs course through their own systems, ending up, finally, in that vast flush, the oceans. Meanwhile, viruses mutate, from Covid-19 to something out of a sci-fi thriller called the Delta Variant, and on to Omicron, threatening to run through the entire Greek alphabet. The latest scourge is Monkey Pox, one more illness in the animal blame-game, like avian and swine flu, parrot and rabbit fever, chicken and cow pox, bovine spongiform encephalopathy, and lupus, named for facial lesions that resemble wolf-bites.

In 2000, a company called Zion Oil made the astonishing claim that their workers were on "a mission from God, commanded by the bible to search for oil in the

Holy Land and in Texas." Is the land holy only because it contains oil? Language has been twisted and corrupted, so much so that we must ask if the fish on the menu is wild or . . . engineered? Even *pandemic*, a corruption of *pan-demos*, "power to all people," no longer announces the goal of freedom for all, but equality of illness for each person, no matter race, gender, ethnicity, sexual preference, and so on: Democracy as contagion.

Today, as we move through the second decade of the twenty-first century, in the wealthiest country in history, a greater number of farm animals get crowded into their pens and cages, while more than half a million of its people live shadow lives sprawled out on the streets, as houseless or homeless cast-offs, the lucky among them stuffed inside camping tents, enduring freezing rain and sub-zero temperatures on America's once bustling and vibrant sidewalks. People fear the down-and-out and the unwashed, their own sense of charity canceled by the fear of the other. Good Samaritans no longer offer help, in the biblical tradition, for the unknown stranger, but now greet each other at Good Sam Clubs, private rest stops for those who travel the country in their huge motor homes. The houseless, possum-dead in the entranceways of fancy stores, get treated as pariahs, for they drive customers away. Poverty on full view repels prosperity. The solution, brutal and barbaric: Remove the lifeless and hapless, the human litter, and ship them somewhere, anywhere. Remove the unsightly from our sight.

Herman Melville knew that soon, in this nation of promise and alleged concern for all its citizens, very little would matter besides money, followed by the desire for more and more money, the great majority of that wealth derived from extracting oil, no longer plundered in the sea, but on land, ripped, with noisy violence, out of the Earth. Such a brutal and radical rupturing of nature could only result in altering the balance of life, triggering diseases, plagues, new strains of cancer, and deadly pollution that encircles the globe.

The rivers and the streams would die first, then the coral beds, kelp beds, and slowly the oceans themselves would gasp for air. Animals, in the ocean and on land, would go extinct in numbers that would bewilder biologists, followed by the death of nature's flying creatures, including the tiniest insects. Antarctic ice, frozen in place for centuries, would melt faster than predicted. Polar Bears would starve to death or drown. People would begin dying in ferocious numbers from diseases undiagnosed or unknown, many of them odd, unpronounceable, or one more mutation of cancer. Certain species of trees, including ancient cactii, like the Joshua Tree, would burn at such intense temperatures that biologists labelled their end as "extinction events." The Great Salt Lake is now a "terminal lake," exposing its huge cache of toxic heavy metals.

Entrepreneurs sounded more and more illogical or deranged, adept in the art of taking apart the Earth, piece by piece—of draining its waterways, changing the direction of its rivers, and levelling its mountains, blasting and excavating until nothing remained but catastrophe, made evident in rising sea levels and record temperatures, in floods and fires of biblical proportions, in shrinking coastlines and expanding deserts. (On February 3, 2023, Mount Washington, in New Hampshire, broke all records: 105 degrees below zero.)

"Global warming," "catastrophe," "eco-horror"—language fails to describe our Postscript. Numbers must suffice: In the Pacific Northwest, temperatures in the summer of 2022 reached a record 116 degrees, too hot and dry for Douglas Firs, in Oregon's primeval forests, to take root, much less reach maturity. No rain fell for four months. Death Valley had record-breaking days that reached 130 degrees, which can damage brains. Children who fell on the summer sidewalks in Phoenix, Arizona, a city that reached 110 degrees for fifty-four days in the July and August of 2023, went to the hospital with third-degree burns.

In Melville's projected and frightening scenario, the so-called Melting Pot of a nation—an image that mocks global warming—in which various ethnicities got stirred about and integrated in the huge cauldron called America, no people would become more elevated than those most responsible for the demise of the Earth, the

Robber Barons of Commerce. They sailed into Plymouth Bay, not on a whaler named for an act of genocide, but on a vessel suggesting spring and renewal, the Mayflower, under the command of Captain Christopher Jones. The Captains of Commerce who followed also had names washed clean of ethnicity: Andrew Carnegie, Jay Gould, William DuPont, Jr., Henry Ford, John Jacob Astor, John D. Rockefeller, John Murray Forbes, and Cornelius Vanderbilt.

In its development and exploitation, its monstrous accumulation of wealth, this country had no use for a definition of civilization, quickly bypassing such a nicety, or racing past the idea altogether—far too busy making money to care about defining itself. Like the cinema, the country created the illusion of speeding up the action, moving from mere nationhood and a grand republic, slipping through the narrow passage of a civil war, moving past the evil of slavery, and hurling itself into a future dominated by the machinery of capitalism.

Melville strips bare people's fascination with a capital economy, in Chapter VI, by having Ahab nail a gold doubloon to the main mast, which as he puts it, became "the ship's navel," the omphalous of wholesale killing for cash. The doubloon, its bright gold head reflecting the sun, would belong to the first person to spot Moby Dick. That lucky person also received the highest honor: the beheading of Moby Dick—capital investment in exchange for capital punishment. Melville chooses one of the most innocent of the crew, the African American cabin boy, Pip, to reveal the meaning of the doubloon.

During Pip's first whale hunt, when the crew had harpooned its initial whale, Pip, suddenly overcome by fear, leaped out of the boat, entangling himself in the lines. He would have drowned had the crew not cut him loose, saving Pip from certain death, but at the cost of losing their whale and thus a good deal of their money.

During the next hunt, Pip leapt out of the boat again, but this time the men did nothing to save him. For a time, he floated and struggled in the vastness of the ocean, until Ahab happened to spot him and pulled him back on board. But Pip seemed to have gone mad—he said that while his body was back on deck, his soul remained in the ocean. The immensity of the sea had revealed to Pip the reality that nothing exists but mere vastness—"The ringed horizon began to expand around him miserably." That the nature of reality is a blank, albino-white like a whale, onto which people must project meaning, drove him into madness—but one quite puny and muted compared with his master Ahab's boundless fury and rage.

And while Pip may have lost his mind, he has gained insight and a vision, an understanding of the way money, as power, controls and destroys. Ishmael believed that Pip had a most profound conversion: "Pip saw God's foot on the treadle of the loom, and spoke it; and therefor his shipmates call him mad." In his altered state, Pip focused his gaze on the doubloon and began an incantation: "I look, you look, he looks; we look, ye look, they look."

Ahab believed Pip was merely parsing sentences, reciting exercises from some grammar book. This was a turning point in Ishmael's own being, as he will later replace the misunderstood Pip, adrift and alone in the open sea. Pip thus explained that everyone—I, he, them, it—in every configuration, was wholly transfixed by money, by its allure, by its kinship with the sun itself. Money is the grammar of action, making connections even with killing. Pip knew the rhetoric of capital, his incantation serving as his Manifesto against the blinding glare of gold.

It is tempting to see Pip as the Shakespearean fool, with Ahab as the mad king, especially given Ahab's response to Pip's seeming nonsense: "And I, you, and he; and we, ye, and they are all bats; and I'm a crow, especially when I stand on top of this pine tree here. Caw! caw! caw! caw! caw! caw! Ain't I a crow? And where's the scare-crow? There he stands; two bones stuck into a pair of trowsers, and two more poked into the sleeves of an old jacket." But Pip is nowhere near fool, or cabin boy, or African American, the lowest rank in the work order, for Melville elevates Pip to the highest level of naked insight, surprising us with his innate wisdom, for on board whaling vessels the dirty work was carried out by an indentured crew, many of them Africans, some freed or escaped slaves, and the gruesome work drove many of them mad. Unnamed and unknown, they carried out the impossibly hard and back-breaking labor on which the success of capitalism rested—labor obviously unfit for the likes of gentlemen farmers—including the tilling, planting, weeding, and watering of row after unending row of cotton. Such lowly labor could only be carried out by those who had been degraded by their skin color, as darkies, or worse, and ultimately condemned as slaves.

What was true on-board whaling ships held for deeply indentured, enslaved workers. On the plantations in the Deep South, West Africans were called anything that reminded one of trash, vermin, or the sub-human. Those workers, who laid the track for the western portion of the seven-hundred-mile Transcontinental Railroad, some fifteen thousand Chinese men and women, had their dignity revoked as mere Coolies. In the forties, on farms in the rich California valley, temporary workers from Mexico were called Brazeros, Spanish for "arms," a slur that reduced a whole human being to their limbs, mere tools for picking grapes, oversprayed with carcinogenic pesticides and herbicides.

All the while, with surrogates doing the damnable work, the newly inscribed entrepreneurs robbed the Earth of its resources, selling off every lump of coal, every ounce of oil, and every office of importance and political clout, along with any other so-called resource, including, in more recent times, plutonium, uranium, silica, and copper, and now lithium and cobalt, to the highest bidder—no questions asked, no backgrounds checked.

In the age of technology, the new silent dynamos that fit on a lap require exotics like terbium and dysprosium, and become humanized by the illusion that they possess memories, language, and a central nervous system called a mother board.

Melville knew that the success of a capital economy demanded that most precious commodity, in its many forms, oil, the harvesting of it from whales reaching its peak around the time he was finishing *Moby Dick*. In 1829, New England registered 203 whaling vessels, while just five years later, the number more than doubled, to 421. By 1840, over 522 ships, barks, and schooners were registered to hunt whales. Six years later, 736 vessels left New Bedford and Nantucket, in Massachusetts; New London, in Connecticut; and Sag Harbor, in Long Island, the average voyage lasting some three years.

In between the production of whale oil and petroleum, two other oils became significant; the first was olive oil. Columbus had brought his caravels to the New World, loaded with oil pressed from olives grown in Italy, then known as "pure oil," now known as "extra virgin." Columbus allotted a daily ration of one quarter of a liter, or approximately one cup, to each crew member, for dressing their tomatoes and pasta.

During the so-called Middle Passage, slave traders brought yet another oil to the New World, the slightly sweet-smelling palm oil. A staple in Africa, people used palm oil from Senegal to Angola. It was so cheap and plentiful that slavers fed it to their captives aboard ship, and rubbed it on their bodies to give them a healthier, younger, more vibrant look, in the hope of that they might fetch higher prices on the auction block. Today, people not only consume more palm oil than any other form of vegetable oil—a whopping seventy-four million tons world-wide in 2022—but manufacturers use it as a base for cosmetics and lipstick, printers' ink, non-stir peanut butter, and in the formulation of biofuel. So much of the Amazon Rain Forest has been burned to the ground to make room for planting oil palms (and raising cattle), some biologists now predict that by 2050 the Amazon will become a savannah.

The destruction of the Earth began with grotesque, serial killing in the oceans, followed by murderous excavation deep within the Earth's bowels—both activities undertaken out of sight and beyond scrutiny and certainly beyond concern. What one cannot see simply does not exist—thus no reason to worry about it—and even what we can see, we know can be a fake. The introduction of the new "anointed machinery" promised a life of ease and luxury. But the shift to a machine-fired, high-speed economy, propelled by the new engines and gadgets of modern life, was clearly a devil's bargain. For, to keep those machines running at full speed, day and night, demanded burning up more and more fossil fuel, resulting in nothing less than the slow death of the natural world. Entrepreneurs considered such destruction as necessary, inevitable, or much worse, of no consequence.

While crude oil may not have been able to anoint, that thick residue conferred the highest status on the entrepreneurs who had enough money, the correct-sounding name, a tough enough will, and the right earth-devouring equipment to rip open the Earth and rob it of its riches, which proved much more useful, much more lucrative than the Holy Oil prized by the Church. Prospectors attacked the land like so many Ahabs, inured to killing, indifferent to beauty, and filled with rage at having to work, even a bit, for their wealth. It is difficult to imagine a more crucial document, one designed to warn of the impending demise of humanity's home, than the Manifesto of Herman Melville.

But its warning is difficult to get at. For the real heart of the book, its deepest political relevance, lives in its dense images and convoluted sentence structures, in Melville's sometimes odd choice of words, a great many of which he seems to have shaken out of an Anglo-Saxon Word-Hoard, overlaid with whaling slang, along with phrases and names either borrowed from the Bible or made up out of holy cloth. His redesigned language has congealed thick enough to inspire its own etymological dictionary, like those guides for the perplexed who slug it out, say, with *Finnegans Wake*. In 1850, for example, *dick* was slang for dictionary, typically a whale-sized tome.

Moby Dick exalts life as something potent and filled with potential, which makes destroying its beauty, magnificence, and meaning particularly perverse. We must beware the coupling of those two impulses—fascination and possession, magnificence and destruction—or, recast more pointedly, when the desire to embrace something beautiful or magisterial gets perverted into the compulsion to smother, or when the idea of loving something, especially oversized, seems so overwhelming that the creature begins to oppress, take over, and to assume far too much, and thus must be eliminated.

Such perversion, of course, degrades the idea of the human and the humane. How to explain the feeling of exaltation toward something so extraordinarily alive devolving into the need to destroy it, sheer delight for life dissolving into intense lust for death. The movement from awe to the awful, from spectacle to sacrifice, reveals itself, most starkly, in the behavior of big-game hunters who, seconds before pulling the trigger, yell or exalt: "What A Beauty! It's huge! Shot it right in the heart!" And so, the lion's head gets mounted on a wall in the den, a sign of the hunter's supposed love of wildlife, but much more serving as a testament to his prowess as a brave, big-game hunter.

It is clear we need more than slogans. We know well the mantrum, "Love the Earth," an imperative borne during the first Earth Day, on April 22, 1970, and still the planet coughs and collapses, on what seems its final days on life support, more than half dead from black lung. Creatures freeze at our sight, sensing certain death; and even the largest of them, like Moby Dick, duck for cover, fleeing for their lives, knowing they are prime targets. The trauma of ripping natural resources out of the Earth's inner core, which takes place outside ethical boundaries, and beyond moral concerns, does not seem much different, in its exaggerations, from killing those most gigantic mammals who dominate the ocean with their wonder, or butchering the largest creatures in the woods that titillate with their chirps and chants.

It is that anomaly, the enigma named Herman Melville, who sent aloft his strange creation, *Moby Dick; or, the Whale,* as a warning to unsuspecting, unprotected readers. The book demands nothing less than a radical change of heart about realigning people's stance in the natural world. There can be no force greater, and certainly no declaration more crucial, than people who have been revulsed by their own greed and behavior, and who find the determination, finally, to lay down their oppressive power and their lame slogans for the protection of the innocent.

Indeed, to be effective, Manifestos must be written from the heart, most evident in those that spring fully formed from eccentric upstarts, to repeat, like the Futurists, Surrealists, and Dadaists. From Marx to Marinetti, from Andre Breton to Stan Brakhage, from Seneca Falls to Oakland, the heart, as master both of conversion and conviction, takes charge over the head, adopts exaggeration over the logical, and takes on tough arguments over bumper-sticker simplicities. It is not the scientist and most decidedly not the neuroscientist, but only the artist who can see the truth, and proclaim it, in words or images to the great majority of us.

In Melville, the word remains elevated, sanctified, alive in plant and person, made so potent by one of its earliest navigators, Homer, revivified by Shakespeare, to whom Melville did not turn until late in the writing of *Moby Dick*, but to whom he then raised hosannas, as if Christ, Himself, had returned: "Ah, he's so full of sermons-on-the-mount, and gentle, aye, almost as Jesus. I take such men to be inspired . . . that this moment Shakespeare in heaven ranks with Gabriel, Raphael, and Michael. And if another Messiah comes, twill be in Shakespere's (sic) person."

Melville may not care about spelling Shakespeare's name correctly, but he knew enough to worm his way inside his sentences and images, to enter into the nature of his characters and the intent of his plotting. Melville especially took to the poetic rants of King Lear who, standing naked on a heath, finds himself howling into an uncaring universe cracked open by hurricanes, lightning, winds, and torrential rain—disasters on Earth ratified by disorder in the heavens. ("As above, so below.") Who can save us? Who can rescue our poor souls—no one less than a Messiah.

That appellation, *Messiah,* which translates as "anointed" (in Hebrew *Mashiach*), is an honorific that got sanctified only with oil. Christ or *Christos,* translates literally as "the anointed one." For their inaugurations, the Israelites poured scented olive oil on the heads of the elected, at times over their entire bodies to ward off evil. The word for *olives* and the *olive tree* (*oleaia*), in Greek, collapses into the single word for oil, *oleus,* suggesting that only one kind of oil mattered. English produces both a redundancy, "olive oil," and the oddity of *petros* ("stone") and *oleus* ("oil") joined as *petroleum*, which can refer only to a miracle of biblical proportions, as in Deuteronomy: "To draw oil from the flinty crag." We also read that Jacob, in Genesis 28, anointed the rock he had used for a pillow while asleep in Canaan with olive oil, elevating the place called Luz, or "turning aside," with Beth-El, "The House of God."

In the more modern period, oil no longer blesses and sanctifies, but in a most irreligious reversal, becomes the stuff of fortunes generated by huge petroleum corporations. *Moby Dick* thus records the history of that most essential element, from something holy—"as rare," Ishmael warns, "as the milk of queens"—to something stripped of mystery and religion, devolving into one more product for someone to peddle for profit. After olives and whales, palms and macassar nuts, came the goo extracted from deep within the interior of the Earth itself, immediately crowned as liquid gold or black gold.

That biblical miracle, petroleum—"oil from rock"— propelled this country into the twentieth century and with astonishing speed into the modern age, pushing life, at the same time, to the brink of total disaster. To repeat: One-hundred corporations now account for seventy-one percent of the world's greenhouse gas emissions—a staggering one trillion tons of CO2 and other poisons released into the atmosphere each year—nearly all those one-hundred corporations in the business of refining petroleum. The top four polluters are Shell, ExxonMobil, Chevron, and BP.

Melville knew oil intimately, from the tiny olive for anointing, to the massive whale for lighting and lubricating. He knew palm oil that people used for cooking, and macassar oil for grooming, and he knew the black gold that had been languishing for millennia deep underground, retrieved and refined into fuel, so that the machines of the new age could run at top speed seemingly forever. The word *fuel,* Greek for "fire," did not enter the language until 1886, inverting the myth of Prometheus, the Titan, who no longer steals fire from the heavens and brings it to Earth in a stalk of fennel as a gift to humankind. Instead, the titans of commerce tear fuel from deep beneath the Earth, haul it above ground as a wonder for humankind, as a gift so poisonous it destroys everything it touches.

In this country, the lust for oil began around 1792 with a handful of shady characters, who began bottling the oil they found floating on top of backyard wells, and on the surface of springs, streams, and rivers, in and around Titusville, Pennsylvania, promoting the sticky goo as a panacea for everything that ailed. Those early mountebanks, using sales-talk slick as their oil, like Melville's Confidence Man, sold their cure-all as bottled holy water, ensuring both bodily health and spiritual well-being.

These new hucksters credited their magical compound, known popularly as "rock oil," with the power of curing and healing and transforming the ordinary into the exquisitely holy. They advertised their new-found miracle in the local newspapers, promoting the power of rock oil to cure cradle cap, soothe diaper rash, eliminate dandruff, soften dry and cracked feet, melt earwax, alleviate constipation, and in the most astounding and broad claim, to deliver salvation to the infant and the elderly. Critics dismissed the claims as akin to the hype of "snake oil," recalling those Chinese workers on the railroad, who drank the oil of water snakes to promote vigor and invite spiritual healing.

"Snake oil salesman" came to describe a generation of slick, fast-talking hucksters, indifferent to the fakery they were hawking, or to any damage they might be inflicting on their customers, as well as on the environment. They siphoned oil from streams and rivers, passing off their heavily hyped product, in bottles adorned with colorful labels, as the latest miracle cure, guaranteeing health, power, and an all-around uplift. "Penn Rock Oil" could make a person feel as powerful as a machine.

One particularly aggressive and fast-talking entre-preneur, who had enjoyed an early and lucrative career selling whale oil, was a con artist named "Colonel" A. C. Ferris. Those who drifted around the edges of power, desperate to make a killing, conferred on them-selves a military rank, commanding instant respect—thus, Colonel Ferris. A slick trickster, Ferris knew that, if he wanted to make a fortune, selling whale-oil door-to-door was small beer. In November of 1857, Ferris quit his Penn Rock pursuit, and launched the first petroleum business in the country, naming it for a local native tribe, the Seneca Oil Company. For Ferris had began exploring for oil on land occupied by the Seneca Nation, founding the petroleum industry in this country, like whaling, cotton, tobacco, and so on, on sacrilege, arrogance, and the exploitation of human beings who had occupied the land long before the arrival of Ferris and his ilk. The Seneca people received no remuneration.

Two years after launching his business, in 1859, Ferris hired another officer manque, Colonel Edwin Drake. This Colonel noticed slicks of oil floating on the surface of local streams and wondered if that might indicate oil deposits underground. He did not wonder for long. For the new assistant at the Seneca Oil Company, who knew nothing about oil exploration, had discovered (or uncov-ered) oil in this country, far outstripping the rush for gold in the 1840s.

On August 27, 1859, Drake drilled this country's first commercial oil well, in a remote spot on the map called Titusville, Pennsylvania. Between 1862 and 1868, Drake built eight refineries in that tiny burgh of Titusville, a place that, during those oil-saturated years, boasted more millionaires per capita than anywhere else in the world. Whale, olive, palm, castor bean, and macassar oil were no match for the thick, black tar that tens of thousands of workers began hauling up from Middle Earth—discovery as utterly transformative, monumentally lucrative, and conclusively deadly. That discovery, eight years following the appearance of *Moby Dick,* sealed our fate. It is our charge to unseal it,

God's bounty—the Earth's enormous fortunes—lay dormant and out of view, just waiting, as the hype would have it, to be liberated from its deep burial sites, needing to be cajoled, forced, and sometimes even bullied above ground, for our needs and pleasure. Edwin Laurentine Drake, an unemployed train conductor, passing himself off as Colonel Drake, founded the empire of oil in this country. For that swindle, the Earth has paid a staggeringly high price.

Those conmen expanded at a rapid pace, and the names proliferated to keep up with their suspect behavior: swindler, scammer, mountebank, rascal, cheater, con-artist, con-man, scamp, scallywag, flimflammer, fraud, sharpie, bilker, and a bit later, the grifter. These bandits of the unabashed included charismatic phonies the likes of which this country had never seen. Those who toyed with people's trust and good-will were legion, and their kind, over the years, multiplied.

With their enormous wealth and oversized personalities, every one of those evangelical preachers manque had received election into the Church. Without exception, they were all white, all East Coast, all native-born. The list excluded those who dared take up lives outside of New England, and all those who had no architect on retainer to design their compounds tucked inside the harbors of Boston or Nantucket. Instead of whaling vessels, the Brahmins boarded massive yachts, leaving Sag Harbor in bliss, having never heard of that fatted book about whaling.

Herman Melville, the loudmouth creator, or perhaps more accurately, the loudmouth perpetrator of *Moby Dick*, is most deliberate in describing, in detail so horrific it repulses, the killing off of the largest specimens of nature imaginable, a horror to which we bear witness through Ahab's willful acts of maniacal retaliation, recounted in Melville's religious language and his own ramped-up outrage over the Grand Kill. People may fall, spirits may dampen, but Melville's language will not be turned aside and certainly not defeated: His words remain elevated and brutally convincing.

All things in *Moby Dick* are oversized, from language to image, from sea to sky, from the distended ego of its captain to the expanded girth of the whale, from the length of sentences to the heft of the book, itself, from the size of the whales to the time it takes, finally, to rob them of their lives. All of it has been amplified and magnified, so that landlubbers might more easily see and hear what takes place out of sight, out of view. In this telling, on such a grand scale, destruction approaches the exaggerations of a Tall Tale, defiled by the blood of a revenge tragedy. *Moby Dick* is oversized, impressive, elusive.

In the order of human destruction, the giants must be killed first. Melville knew this well: First, the killing of those oversized whales and then, by the middle of the nineteenth century, when entrepreneurs moved their campaign of wholesale slaughter onto the land, the leveling of ancient Redwoods, some over two thousand years old and over 200 feet tall. So fierce and so efficient was the felling of trees that in the span of twenty years, between the 1830s and 1850s, ninety-five percent of the old growth trees, mostly Douglas Firs, were cut and shipped to other countries as building material. Too many species of fish, as well as the bison, and a whole slew of birds, would all follow in a well-disciplined regime of execution.

The first band of sawyers, formulated as the Tinsman Company, began operating as early as 1785, in a small burgh in Pennsylvania, proudly named for its industry of destruction, Lumberville. Fifty years after the founding of the Tinsman Company, lumber had become a most lucrative industry, with scores of companies across the country intent on levelling trees—again, the largest first—as swiftly as possible. Entrepreneurs in nearby Titusville, the birthplace of oil, alert to easy money, also built some 17 saw mills, cutting down what grew locally, hemlocks and pines. Over a mere twenty years, close to two million acres of forest in the Pacific Northwest—California, Oregon, and Washington—were left to rot as stumps, emblems of what once had been.

The felling of various trees took with it scores of animals and birds, unseen but that made their nests and secured their food, in and around those trees—from the tops of the Douglas Firs to the roots of the Redwoods. In short order, the Northern Spotted Owl, the Marbled Murrelet, the Black-Tailed Deer, Black Bear, Bald Eagle, bobcat, coyote, the Humboldt Marten, the Red-Tailed Vole, and myriad varieties of chipmunks, squirrels, rodents, flies, butterflies, and large, colorful moths, like the Pitch, the Sphinx, the Combat, and the spectacular variegated orange/black moth, all totally disappeared. The two greenest regions in the country, Georgia and the Pacific Northwest, combined forests, in 1948, to found the largest lumber and paper company in the world, aptly named Georgia-Pacific.

We must read this anomaly, Melville, at his highest and most potent level, sounding his own loud and raucous warning about the obsessive drive of the monied class to destroy every last vestige of the environment. Melville's warning, would be the only one of its kind until a century later, when environmental writers would issue their early warnings, in the sixties about polluted air and water. Since then, key corporations have been so intent on getting rich that they have taken apart the Earth, and while we are all not responsible, we are all implicated, left with the unimaginable horror of the end of history, left with a suffocating choice—whether to describe the demise of the Earth in this or that particular way. We have been left with the most enormous responsibility imaginable: To restore all organic life to a state of health. It is a tale that can be told only once, for life is fast coming to a conclusion.

And so, in what appears more and more to be end days, who can be expected to care about details? Again: A handful of corporations are destroying the natural world so thoroughly that its insidiousness infects every crack and cranny of the created world, in places where no one has ever trod as well as where humans have left a heavy footprint. Pollution and poisoning are so pervasive, persistent, and insidiously invisible that corporations were able to contaminate the heart and lungs of the planet, its arterial and venous systems, without alarm until people got sick and too many of them died.

Pray for the large beasts and for the smallest creatures. Protect them all. Melville encourages us to root for the whale, to cheer its escape and its safe return home. Why should things be otherwise? Why would anyone wish anything different? Hands off the Sperm whale and back off from the Giant Sequoia. Obey the sign that hangs over all of creation: DO NOT DISTURB! The oceans of the world are the places where the whales belong, and alive and healthy is what their condition must be.

But whales now feed on facsimiles of food, so that instead of ingesting shrimp, they filter through their baleen passages, or grind up in their toothy mouths a million bits, daily, of shimmering plastic. In addition, every species of whale still gets hounded, relentlessly, for its many precious commodities to satisfy the wealthy. How disgraceful to dissect the whale, using its bodily fluids to concoct high-end perfume, its bones to keep corsets snug, its flesh to make fancy sushi, and most repulsive, its innards to grind into pet food. Cargo ships run over them in seemingly a sport, killing 20,000 each year. Hundreds more die from the loud and noisy propellors of huge container ships and luxury liners, as well as the dreaded military sonar. The cargo ship, Emma Maersk is longer than four football fields. To move that beast through the water requires a propeller that stands over thirty-feet high, with six blades, and weighs an astonishing 131 tons, more than a house. In full spin, the noise is horrific, some 190 decibels: Imagine creatures of the sea forced to sit next to a gigantic speaker at a heavy metal concert. At any given time, there are some 60,000 commercial ships moving through the oceans, most of them at full speed. Hawthorne is dead. In his absence, who will shout, over the din of commerce and with his ear-shattering thunder, that great, affirming NO?

Moby Dick may have a name but he must not be construed to belong to anyone. The whale is not a commodity or someone's domesticated pet. Its name in Hebrew, *Livyatan*, means "the coiled one." For Plato, naming must reveal essence rather than possession. Even Ishmael's name, which we have conferred on him, is only on loan—from us to him, from bible to biography, from his appearance to his disappearance. When the narrative ends, and his condition changes, Ishmael and his identity will both evaporate, his identity and essence repossessed.

Melville wrote as if he knew that, as a people, we set out on a journey doomed by our own actions unless we took Ahab's vicious treatment of the whale as a universal lesson, emblematic of the mistreatment and maltreatment of the Earth's many creatures. Again, it is Melville's uncanny prescience to know that if he were going to be heard and effect change, he would have to write well beyond the confines and themes of the expected, in a form that could be emphatic without being didactic, in a style that was critical without being suffocating, with a stance that was urgent without being totally alarming. He had little option but, once again, to write in that politically outspoken and demanding genre, the Manifesto, which demanded nothing short of saving the natural world.

Melville's tough-to-get-through sentences carry enough explosive charge to blast open the clichés of

American assumptions, revealing history's gritty truth, especially those events enshrined as America's touted successes. Melville brings us so close to the real that we bear witness to the gruesome details about the way morals and ethics, in mid nineteenth-century America, could get so easily cast aside in favor of success and wealth.

Such a grim reality unfolded in the most distorted way, in Melville's description of the routine of serial killing on the high seas, at a level and kind of destruction not yet witnessed on the land, but which would take place with such vengeance that, even with exploitation fully on view, with derricks, pumps, and pipelines, people would dismiss such cruel treatment of the Earth as the price of progress. We once needed more and more whale oil. A bit later, people had to have unlimited amounts of black gold—petroleum.

Greed bred more entrepreneurs, and the Earth shuddered, the constellations took a step back. The bright blue waters grew fetid and turned brown, clarity giving way to the opaque, and then fell to pure muck. The air filled with invisible poisons, making it dangerous to inhale. People fell ill, many died. The dreaded diagnosis: Cancer. Cancer Research UK now lists some 200 different strains. Who could imagine that living could become lethal; that we must be on guard—always—trusting no one? The smallest incursions have caused the largest disruptions.

The catastrophe has arrived, with more and more people utterly frightened, shattered, coping with the unspeakable—the end of our world. Despair, to repeat, has gripped young people in particular, the ones who are supposed to feel invincible and joyous. The news smothers hope: Temperatures soaring and fires blazing, followed by drought, flood, tornadoes, dust-storms, ice storms, hurricanes, ice-quakes, and desertification. We pray and hope while the Earth, exhausted, threatens to call it "quits." The new techno-centi-billionaires tout spaceships to Mars as the new cure-all.

The shiny lure of amassing fortunes always catches the eye of the huckster—money as glittering lure. One of the most successful hawkers of "rock-oil," far outstripping Colonel Ferris, was a conman with a most recognizable family name, William Avery Rockefeller, the father of John Davidson Rockefeller. Beginning in the early 1850s and through most of the 1860s, he passed himself off as Doctor William Levingston, selling brightly colored water as "CURE-ALL," and later "NUJOL," for the whopping price of twenty-five dollars, the equivalent, at the time, of two-months' pay for most Americans. (Plough, Inc. still produces a mineral oil of the same name.)

Rockefeller's two sons, John Davidson and William Avery, Jr., followed their father in fleecing the elderly and the sick, aware early on of the fortunes that could be had in exploiting the industrial, lucrative side of oil. In 1863, in Cleveland, Ohio, four years following the success of Seneca Oil, the brothers founded the Standard Oil Company. John Davidson, who would become the

wealthiest person in this country, became the first entre-
preneur to be promoted from "snake-oil salesman" to
"Robber Baron."

Seven years later, on January 10, 1870, John Davidson
and William Avery Rockefeller removed themselves from
the possibility of personal litigation for poisoning the
environment by transforming Standard Oil into a specter
called a *corporation*, a ghost entity, protecting their
amoral acts of destruction from punishment through
legal immunity called "limited liability," encouraging the
brothers to do with the biosphere whatever they desired.

By discorporating as human beings into the corporation called Standard Oil, John Davidson and William
Avery Rockefeller became ghosts that would refuse to die,
pursuing a dispirited life, free of all values and morals,
free to do what they wished and wanted. Workers for
Standard Oil, using explosives, dredging machines, and
massive drills, forced out of the Earth, year after year,
millions of barrels of petroleum, or crude oil which, when
refined, fired up the machinery of the new era of rapidly
expanding wealth, progress, and prosperity. Unbelievable
quantities of oil were needed to keep the country firing
on all cylinders.

Standard Oil met the challenge, and only too well: By
1878, the Standard Oil Corporation was producing 95
percent of the oil in the country, at a cost of destroying
100 percent of the environment. No one noticed, but
Standard Oil saturated the air with poisons, tainted the

aquifers with poisons, destroyed the Earth with poisons. By issuing stock certificates, Americans could purchase a piece of the corporation, making it impossible, in the most twisted logic, to hold any single individual— CEO, CGO, CFO—responsible for poisoning the environment, and for stockholders to make money off the destruction of their own home.

In killing the first creatures mentioned in Genesis, humans assumed command over light and life. In the new age of De-creation, one must learn to disregard the adverse side effects of every so-called scientific, medical, and technological advance, which meant the fossil fuel that produced the new light and fired the new machines also began, slowly but most assuredly, to blot out the sun and all organic life. It took centuries before anyone mentioned that those changing weather patterns actually were the death throes of the planet. In the end, science and technology had led to darkness and death. Such irony is obviously bizarre, but fatal for everything and everyone.

Nothing stopped the killing of whales. With certain species, like the Baleens, it increased, for their flesh contained more triglycerides, which, when rendered, produced a fattier oil than any of the other species, that burned more brightly and with more animation, more appealing for many people than the focused glow of incandescence. They were also favored by harpooners: Unlike Bowhead and Sperm whales, Baleens moved at far slower speeds, were more docile, and thus easy targets, assuring harpooners of a kill. Again, because of their high levels of fat, once they were killed, they floated, ready for butchering without the mess of having to haul them on board. Docility spelled their undoing, making Baleens hunted nearly out of existence, high on the list of endangered species. The news is grim for the Right whale, also a Baleen, which can grow to over fifty feet, and live for seventy years for, in all the oceans, they number around 360.

It has been illegal to buy whale oil in this country only since 1972, when the U.S. banned commercial whaling. General Motors continued using sperm whale oil in automatic transmissions because, as its engineers argued, whale oil retarded rust, allowing transmissions to operate efficiently throughout the life of their warranty. Flaunting the ban, General Motors used more than 14 million kilos of sperm whale oil yearly, until the federal government invoked a provision of the Endangered Species Act, forcing them to give up the practice in 1973.

By the middle of the nineteenth century, ships were moving by steam-power and harpoons were being fitted with explosive warheads. American whaling vessels sailed throughout the oceans of the southern hemisphere killing easy targets, such as the Baleens, in shocking numbers: 725,000 Fin whales over seventy years. Against such ferocious slaughter, Helen Caldicott issues her own warning: "We stand on the brink of extinction unaware that our time on this precious lump of rock in the endless universe is almost certainly to come to an end." Forty years ago, Calidcott's words may have sounded like exaggerations from an exciteable, perhaps even mad person. Today, they echo as a blistering condemnation.

Can we imagine that, in the middle of the nineteenth century, the natural world was already flirting with extinction and inching closer to the edge of catastrophe by killing whales and robbing them of their oil? This profound desecration constituted the first but enormous step toward the death of the natural world. Meville saw that unfolding with horror and reported it with indignation. In the 1820s, in 2023 adjusted dollars, whale oil sold for $200/barrel, each barrel holding 42 gallons. By 1855, sperm whale oil had reached its highest price, in adjusted figures, at a staggering $1,500/barrel, or $36 per gallon.

Reading by oil lamp was a luxury. In 1846, kerosene was discovered, followed by the kerosene lamp in 1853. By the early 1860s, kerosene, which emits very little carbon monoxide, was sold for $90/barrel or two dollars a gallon. Around that same time, in 1860, the OED records a momentous shift in the meaning of the word *oil*. Oil no longer referred solely to the holy olive or to various nuts and flowers, but almost exclusively to the black tar retrieved from the bowels of the Earth. From the first moments of hauling goo from deep under the ground, people venerated oil as a discovery more important than anything anyone could imagine, an exotic substance holy enough to anoint the lords of commerce.

And so, one is tempted to say, as oil goes, so goes the soul of the nation. As the holy or sacred nature of oil got stripped away, exploited as something essential and necessary by those insistent on amassing fortunes, the sacred in all of nature was also eradicated. With steam replaced by petroleum, whale oil by electricity, and the roar of machines by the silence of the computer, the mechanical/technological revolution would become the most powerful religious movement imaginable, displacing the Church. In the age of technological superiority, supplicants in the first decades of the twenty-first century would no longer orient themselves toward the East, but toward the West, and a bit north, in obeisance to Silicon Valley. Henry Adams could have no idea about the morphing of that first deafeningly loud dynamo into the hum of a computer; of human memory into gigabytes and terabytes; of the sanctified word into the algorithm; of knowledge into mere information.

By the end of the 1850s, whale oil had become too expensive and impractical, and even the fatted oil from Bowhead and Right whales flickered too much for easy reading, burned at too high a temperature, and much too quickly. Whale oil was a luxury. By the 1880s, streetlamps and living rooms were being lit by gas. Oil left the house and moved into the great outdoors. Following its discovery in Titusville, rock and coal oil almost immediately ousted whale oil and kerosene. By the early 1870s, Standard Oil had truly installed itself as the standard, reducing the price of crude oil to about $20/barrel, or fifty cents a gallon. But the most dramatic event in the discovery of oil had yet to take place.

The trajectory of whale oil, to kerosene, to rock oil, to the puny derrick at Titusville, came to an explosive and dramatic climax two years after Melville's death, through yet another mountebank, the self-appointed military officer, Captain Anthony Lucas. After noticing bits of oil floating in the local streams, Lucas erected a crude, wooden derrick, eighty-four feet tall in Beaumont, Texas. As if to mark the new millennium, on January 10, 1901, most appropriately, Lucas—"Bringer of Light"—hit the first gusher and illuminated the world.

Like the contents of an ancient tomb pried open after eons, oil erupted over 150 feet in the air, at the unbelievable rate of 100,000 barrels a day, requiring crews to work around the clock for nine days in order to cap it. Following the first week of the first year of the twentieth century, petroleum took charge over all else. Out of the bottle, the Genie was eager to display its mighty, feisty power. Such a force could never be stuffed back in place, never turned aside. Most destructive of all, people would demand more and more oil for their new machines.

The new century thus opened with a most startling image. Like the mighty Moby Dick, unable to hold its breath a second longer, breaching the surface and blowing water hundreds of feet above its massive body, deep drilling forced crude oil, dormant for millennia, to burst through the crust of the Earth, with geyser-like power and whale-like fierceness. It was a noisy, noxious, and impressive show of industrial potential that reached great heights. In concert with the new Age of the Internal Combustion Engine, the Age of Petroleum had arrived, turning ever more enormous, ferocious, and powerful.

In those very first weeks of the very new century, the United States, with a single image, had proclaimed itself as the world power—crude oil would become the first trillion-dollar industry, raising the banner of capitalism for the rest of the world to witness and salute. Petroleum became the supreme driver of the new economy and the twentieth century marked the beginning of the *petroculture era.*

Given its most sacred, healing, and underground history, people did more than believe in the power of oil. Despite oil's toxicity, the thrill of discovery, the fiery brilliance of the exciting and the new burned so brightly that it attracted thousands of entrepreneurs who, like so many moths, flew into the flame, so transfixed by striking it rich they hardly noticed that they were on fire. Turning away from a near total dependence on whale oil did nothing to halt the slaughter of the largest whales. The sperm whale continued to be hunted, tortured, and killed for its ambergris and thick baleen. Crews continued to kill whales to supply the burgeoning Japanese market for pet treats, for expensive and exclusive sushi restaurants, and for the most recent food innovation on the island, vending machines that dispensed nigiri and hand-rolls of thick whale flesh.

One social and political reformer, a nineteenth-century radical and early outspoken defender of the environment, Henry Shakespear Stephens Salt, read *Moby Dick* as a bold warning about the destruction of nature. Born in India in 1851, the same year that *Moby Dick* was published, Salt became a proselytizing vegetarian, a pacifist, a prison reform activist, and a mentor to a very young Gandhi, tutoring him on non-violent resistance strategies. Salt left his teaching mastership at Eton to pursue a life dedicated to environmental justice and animal rights through social activism.

Salt read *Moby Dick* and found inspiration and guidance. In 1889, two years before Melville's death, and with *Moby Dick* long out of print, Salt took the radical step of reviewing *Moby Dick* for the *Scottish Art Review*. He called Melville the most misunderstood writer of the period and the only true naturalist who was able to conjure stories on behalf of those who cannot speak our language, helping to give meaning to innocent, sentient creatures. The images Salt chose for his review reveal his affection for Melville and his work: "Instead of a landsman's grey-goose quill, he seems to have plucked a quill from a skimming curlew, or to have snatched it, a fearful joy, from a hovering albatross, if not from the wings of the wind itself."

For Salt, Melville wrote from deep within the creases and crevices of nature, deep within his affinity for the so-called dumb and the dumbstruck. By implication and because of his range, Melville managed to command a position high aloft, where the albatross flies, and higher yet, where winds whip and whirl and meaning is known less through logic and more through lilt. Melville chose the quill, Salt so gleefully tells us, so his ideas could soar in the way Homer's "winged words" flew from the mouth of the rhetor.

Melville created sentences with a score, tales that resound as high-pitched song. It must be so, for Ishmael, like a mature Huckleberry Finn, is illiterate. Like Huck, he must talk his tale into being. Without quill or ink, Ishmael taps into some preternatural language. The wind is blowing, which means that Ishmael has to be yelling. It is freezing cold, which means that he must be shivering, alive at the top of his lungs, akin to his creator, Melville. Our narrator is supposed to be dying, but he surprises us by continuously floating and remaining fully alert.

Salt went on to celebrate the unusual style and method of *Moby Dick,* and Melville's uncanny way of entering the life of a whale: "The book is a curious compound of real information about whales in general and fantastic references to this sperm-whale, in particular that 'portentous and mysterious monster,' which is studied (as the bird is studied by Michelet) in a metaphysical and ideal aspect—a mass of tremulous life, all obedient to one volition as the smallest insect."

Two years after his review and the same year that Melville died, 1891, Henry Salt founded the most radical organization for its time, the Humanitarian League. The group was devoted to a single principle: "It is iniquitous to inflict avoidable suffering on any sentient being." At the end of the nineteenth century, in the commercial heart of proper men and women living in the prosperous city of London, the Humanitarian League established itself as a noisy, unruly group committed to the rights of non-humans.

With Melville as his inspiration, Salt managed to persuade such key literary figures as Thomas Hardy and George Bernard Shaw to join, along with the mystic Annie Besant, the Utopian socialist Edward Carpenter, the well-known writers John Galsworthy, Leo Tolstoy, and Thomas Hardy, the British suffragette Christabel Pankhurst, and a fascinating figure named Edith Carrington, a very vocal and very literate activist for animal liberation, who made it her life work to oppose the radically conservative entomologist, Eleanor Anne Ormerod, an extremist determined to rid the Britsh Isles of all things flying.

Drawing on *Moby Dick* for his own style and presentation, Salt published the group's beliefs as The Manifesto of the Humanitarian League, founded on "a high and positive system of morality in the conduct of life, in all its aspects," refusing to "inflict suffering, directly or unintentionally, on any sentient being." The League opposed corporal and capital punishment, hunting, vivisection, and agitated to ban the selling of furs and feathers, both immensely popular at the time for the fashionable dresser.

The Manifesto held fast to what Salt called "the creed of kinship," in staunch opposition to "the wanton ill-treatment of the lower animals." Members articulated their own views on the nature of nature in the League's journal, *The Human Review*, published from 1900 to 1910, replaced by *The Humanitarian*, which remained in publication for nearly two decades, from 1902 until 1919, which marked the end of the League itself.

Beyond all his efforts toward social reform and justice, Salt stands out as one of the first and most powerful advocates for the rights of non-humans, as well as for a movement dedicated specifically to the rights of all sentient beings. He makes a bridge between the nineteenth-century advocates of the rights of animals and the more modern period. Salt's intellectual heir, the philosopher of bioethics and animal liberation, Peter Singer, wrote the preface to Salt's *Animal Rights: Considered in Relation to Social Progress* (1892).

Imagine, then, being so keenly alive and alert to the wonder of sentient life that, when Jules Michelet refers to birds as the "embryo souls" of human beings, nobody laughs, but instead they take delight in his appreciation of the essential language of nature. Herman Melville's *Moby*

Dick must be read in that same spirit, a wizard writing of the created world as something animate and animated, as personal and potently alive, as something he dearly loves and thus aims, most fervently, to protect. Against that view, Melville places a bloody and gratuitous brutality, an environmental calamity hiding behind the name of whaling, a preoccupation forged out of an obsession for profit so blinding it disregards care and ethics, favoring a criminal-like brutality delivered with maniacal force against some of the most majestic animals in nature.

Set aside the thrills and hype of riding high on the waves, and one sees whaling as a business intent on removing the wondrous and majestic, the singular in nature, by carving its flesh into bits for soap and sushi at extraordinary profits. As Melville believed, whaling is little more than concerted killing, enabled by the demands of a capital economy, insulated by the law, encouraged by the marketplace. In the public square, such criminal behavior might result in imprisonment or capital punishment.

All of this devastation and gross torturing has been underscored, vindicated, if you will, by a belief that certain human beings have been directed, through some higher authority, to exploit and destroy the majesty that is nature or the majestic that inheres in all of nature. Worse yet, it is as if God had commanded certain of His elect to eradicate the rest of sentient life, to subsume the bounty of the Earth for their very own needs and desires. Such thinking culminates in rounds of unthinkable violence delivered against the whale as something larger, mightier, more perplexing than everything else. The whale moves about in its habitat incessantly hounded, its majestic size signaling its fate.

Mysterious, bewildering, and far too miraculous for most people, the whale is elusive and unsettling, difficult to distinguish male from female, mammal from fish, species from genus, whether it has teeth or a baleen plate. One can only catch a glimpse of it, and only once in a great while. Nonetheless, the whale is a miracle tarnished. The wonder of whales became the supreme prize in the perversity of wholesale slaughter, as if it begged to be hunted down, finished off, and sold in the marketplace to the eager.

More than most creatures, then, the whale lives a most precarious life. Killing it is a victory like no other, a triumph over the first and most colossal in nature, with the bonus of a person being paid for the kill. Such brutal destruction was not confined to the ocean. In *Of Wolves and Men*, an account of the glory of all wild things, Barry Lopez, projects that between 1850 and 1900, a staggering one to two million were killed on the Great Plains. Lopez offers this tamped-down explanation for such a grotesquerie: "I think it is that we simply do not understand our place in the universe and have not the courage to admit it." It is an explanation that, unfortunately, permits people to leap off the hook of guilt, and to escape blame and punishment much too easily.

The massive and wanton killing of so many wild animals must go beyond a mere "misunderstanding." Surely, the motivation is more deliberate, complicated, and pathological, and one that desires to eradicate everything in nature, especially all that appears majestic, all that we cannot hope to be. Our need to destroy may be enmeshed in the fact that as human beings we fall so mightily short, in so many categories, compared to the kings of the kingdom. The impulse to destroy and kill, often out of the thrill of the so-called sport, and at other times out of what can only be understood as envy of the beautiful and the majestic, must arise from some place in the deepest underbelly of our being.

At this point we might be tempted to say, like Lopez, that rather than compassionate, rightly cautious play-mates eager to interact with the rest of the animate world, we have become wanton killers bent on destroying all of life. Do we only live *on* this Earth and not *in* or *within* it; must we really stand so far outside the natural world, Ahab-like and, for various and never rational reasons, take revenge on all that thrives?

Melville sends us a charge: Bring such arrogance to a halt. The surge of enthusiasm generated by invention and progress blinded us to our place in nature, making us believe, with great conviction, that we had been elected to seize control of the created world, to manipulate it at will, alter and improve it, with such arrogance we could not realize that such a stance was both absurd and dangerous. We have mistaken the luxury of being in nature for the thrill of lording over nature, from being a part of it all to dismantling all of it.

Whaling in America began in the early 1600s and did not end, officially, until 1971—close to four hundred years of professional, wanton slaughtering. On January 10, 1901, when oil gushed from the ground at Spindletop, big business was already adept at killing the natural and feigning ignorance of the deadly side effects. The explosive force of that gusher blew open the doors to enormous profits, world power, and horrific environmental disaster; it shut the doors to knowing nature as anything other than potentialities in the marketplace.

During 1901, Spindletop produced 3.5 million barrels. One year later, the same well was delivering a staggering 17,420,949 barrels a day, enough crude oil to satisfy demands across the country. The phrase, "go ahead, sue me," reverberates with meaning today, for liability is simply the cost of progress, that is, part of the business of ravaging the Earth. Because of Justice Shaw, corporations are content paying the fines for their corrupt behavior, for damage, or even the deaths that they may have caused, as their profits have reached the stratosphere.

Far too many people, from far too many corporations, believe that they occupy a primary and commanding place over the destiny of nature and that all living creatures have been created, either for their pleasure or for their gain: Everything and anything can be exploited. We do not need courage to understand our place in the universe. We need the courage to change our minds about what our place has devolved into, and the will to take up a position that is more hallowed and sacred—more reasonable, tamped down and refined, more natural and in line with a modesty in the face of such majesty that the sentient world, with all of its seemingly limitless number of creatures, offers to us. Confronted with the miraculous, we need humility.

As the Right whale and Northern Spotted Owl move closer to extinction, we may not hear a single sound of anguish, and we may not see a single act of protest, but we must realize the incredibly deep and painful suffering of creatures being forced, slowly or rapidly, to depart this planet forever. We need the courage—and, these days, it takes a good deal of it—to return to the very basic belief that all things are sacred and thus sanctified.

In what might be the mightiest sci-fi or fantasy tale of all time, Herman Melville chose a huge whale to awaken his readers to the wonder that pervades all of nature. Not many writers could muster the courage to pull off such a Manifesto against such a mighty and far-fetched subject as the destruction of the natural world, and few could see the horrific end-result of such exploration and expansion. And yet, there was Melville, one-hundred and seventy years ago, describing the spread of unchecked greed on the high seas just before that criminal behavior washed ashore, anticipating something as dire as the end of the natural world. He knew that greed could not be contained, that it would expand beyond the oceans and infect the land and all things living. Melville did that unabashedly, and he did it with great daring, before both the full effect of chaos and the most unreal levels of destruction became obvious.

Melville must thus be seen as more than an author, and more than someone who is writing in the midst of a crisis he knew would only get much more virulent. Herman Melville is a champion of life. Henry Salt perceived that fact and honored Melville's conviction. Perhaps, in the middle of the nineteenth century, as witness to the near extinction of the wolf, the bison, and the total extinction of the passenger pigeon, along with so many other species, as well as thousands of Native Americans, any writer possessed of right reason must become a defender of the natural world, and some, like Melville, more intense and more insistent than others.

Melville had already witnessed the spectacular Stellar's Sea Cow, a creature weighing close to ten tons, a megafauna survivor from the Pleistocene, pass without notice into extinction. First described in 1741, it took less than thirty years before fur traders, hunting for sea otters, had killed them all. The demise of the Stellar's Sea Cow, as so-called collateral damage in the making of hats, sweaters, purses, and scarves out of otters, prompted contemporary biologists to initiate the science of extinction. Melville knew, he lamented, and he wrote. He grew angry and he wrote some more. He grew desperately angry, eager to turn readers into activists. Place him in a separate category, for Melville is brave and outspoken, possessed of a demanding vision. We need to pay attention to his well-formed outrage—especially now. And, with a bit of prodding, we must pay homage to Herman Melville by trying to do more than merely putting a halt to environmental desecration.

We must try to reinvigorate people's imaginations so that they see the wonder that inheres, not only in the majestic whale, but also in the tiny but miraculous Bartailed Godwit, that can migrate 7,000 miles without landing. Large or small, the stakes remain the same—a heart-pounding aliveness of myriad creatures. To get us to embrace the ordinary, Melville forced us to stare at the tormented life of the extraordinary.

There must be a superfund cleanup for the mind and the imagination, one that allows us to adopt, perhaps for the very first time, the roles of steward and stewardship, of gardener and guardian; that permits us to realize that, after all these years, with enough effort our greed can be turned aside. Imagine us as easy-going beings that can be bowled over, overwhelmed, knocked-out by the sheer wonder of whales, by the sound of the smallest bee, or by a bud unfolding in the earliest moments of spring.

The holy status with which the whale entered the world on the fifth day of creation did not deter the editors of the *OED*, in their first edition, in 1884, from defining it in a most shocking, unbelievable way, as little more than just another commodity in a seeming endless list of unnatural resources, sounding as if a whaling captain had concocted the definition: "Any of the large fish-like marine mammals of the order *Cetaciea,* which have forelimbs like fins and a tail with horizontal flukes, and are hunted for their oil and whalebone."

The definition banishes all ethical considerations, the editors not pausing to add or even imply that hunting and killing whales for their oil and other body parts was a huge commercial enterprise, or that because it has been so much hounded and hunted by trained assassins, the whale faces extinction. The definition is an absurdity: If it is a whale, it must be hunted down and killed.

The editors do not lament such a sorry and sordid plight. They do something even stranger. By damning that animal, they come very close to condemning it, by very definition, to a life of eternal pursuit and persecution, reducing all whales to huge, water-locked natural resources, as if being hunted down and killed for their oil were part of the whale's altruistic DNA. The entry in the *OED* implies that hunting down and killing the whale, as if it were some natural resource, does not reside in the arrogance or greediness of people, or in the brutality that drives capitalism, but in the unfortunate constitution of the animal itself. As a kind of floating commodity, the whale invites its own demise.

We cannot hope to reorder our priorities until we can view the created world as miraculously alive and astonishingly complex, charged with holiness, or at least infused with a huge dose of the wild and the wonderful. One does not have to believe in God, or even in a divine order of creation, but if we are to be pulled back from the brink of extinction, we must treat all living things as wondrous, miraculous, and inviolable.

We would do well to believe, like Henry Salt, that to do harm to anything wild and alive is unforgivable and irredeemable; that to level the least bit of harm is to condemn a living thing—tree or trout, badger or bee—to continuous pain and to consign the torturer to a life diminished. We must celebrate the differences that distinguish us from the animal world and rejoice in the similarities that bring us up close to snouts and snapping.

We must know, and we must respect, that those myriad animals inhabit their own, very complex spaces and behave in their own, most singular ways, which seem so puzzling to us. They might at first glance appear to have little or nothing to do with us and with our own very complicated and sophisticated lives, but as they carry out their precise acts in and among each other, they implicate us in their protection and thus in their well-being.

We must further understand that the word *resource,* implying some eternal supply of manna, from some heavenly font, is a farce that has brought us to disaster. We have consumed nature's bounty at a most rapid clip and can no longer dip into a pot of riches that we believe will magically replenish. The term *resource* is not merely a fiction, but a most dangerous lie, for neither oil, nor gas, can re-source or replenish itself. The same is true, obviously, of fish and frogs, wolves and trees. The same is not true of goodwill.

The true resource, the one we so affectionately call Mother Earth, having endured far too much exploitation, neglect, and abuse will simply run dry of abundance. She will not withhold, but one day soon, she will be stripped of all riches. Mother Earth will turn into Old Mother Hubbard, for the arrow on the gauge of all gauges, at this moment, points very close to empty— not a single bone to be found in the cupboard. The whirring, diamond-fitted drill will soon bore deep into the marrow of the Earth, but not a drop of oil will rise to the surface; the lakes will fill with silt, the rivers run brown, all salmon will be hatched in concrete pools, all mussels grown on ropes, all oysters born from seeds; genetically-modified apples will remain forever red and ripe, lacking flavor—all that was once bright green now an eternal sepia. We bear witness to a disaster that our economy cannot support, for capitalism cannot succeed without people believing in a future tense, and can only satisfy that belief in the future with an unending supply of raw materials. Only profit matters, only the bright and promising future tense signifies, only the bottom line defines.

One can but wonder just what our attitude toward the Earth will be once it runs dry of its natural and unnatural resources. Will we still call it the Earth? Will we come to resent, or even condemn this globe we live on? Will we punish it even more than we do now? Will we carry out our sullen lives on what is the thin skin of utter disappointment? Will we even have so-called lives? For those invested heavily in making a fortune from its largesse, the reaction might truly be anger, rage, and even outrage. Or, more Ahab-like, it will be classical rage that will lead, first, to a demand for revenge, followed by horrific backlash, the side-effect of total destruction that destroys the ship of state and all on-board.

Those who remain might apologize for the catastrophe caused by human insatiability, ask for forgiveness to . . . whatever/whoever is left to hear us out. Or perhaps we, too, all of us alive at this moment, might vanish. No one truly knows. Covid-19 has given us a glimpse of what the future might feel and look like when people finally get aroused and grow alarmed about the end of life; about the arrogance of experimental science, and the ignorance of just how lethal a virus can get; about where it came from and where it is headed; about whether it exists or is just another conspiracy dreamed up by the so-called Deep State to keep us as docile agents of despair. Or is Covid now as ubiquitous and hearty as the common cold, here to stay and, perhaps, to mutate into a stronger strain?

By suffocating the imagination with its descriptions of cruelty—against humans, animals, and nature writ large—Melville says, No More! In reading that book, we catch ourselves eavesdropping on the most horrendous and primitive, the most unbelievable and disgusting scenes of dissection, dismemberment, and de-creation of living, breathing, oversized, miraculous, and most holy creatures—acts of sheer violence that cause animals to die in the most unimaginable ways.

In what other tales of adventure do we read and weep because of such overarching fear and pain? We move through Melville with disgust, powerless to defend against it, for Ishmael keeps the killing alive in the imagination. And again, we turn to our own plight in this threatened world: How to stop the decapitation of nature? The last act in the book, Ishmael's rescue, is one of kindness and compassion, of generosity by a Good Samaritan.

By making us bear witness to the cruelty of whaling, Melville implicates us in its horror. We are present at the drawing board of all things human and inhuman, clearing a place from which we can witness ourselves stripped bare of all convention and all manner of manners. What a clash: Holy creatures helpless against the assault by commercial killing. At the ground zero of our being, we might ask, is this what it means to be alive, to kill sentient creatures, in disregard of their glory, in order to be able to cook, to read, to look good, and smell even better? Does comfort require such violence, such outright terror, such sacrilege?

Does our luxury demand the destruction of the entirety of the natural world, turning us mean and vicious, encouraging us to kill, in turn, and without caring? Are we merely an array of barbarians, congregating at the gates, anxious to take over and take charge? We must put up our hands and surrender. The times are dire. In our faces, nature sends up its own defiance: NO IN THUNDER!

One wonders, then, and such a suggestion must be taken most seriously, if we as a people can ever regain our ability to be so dazzled once again by the natural world that we could never think of killing a single thing; if we can ever reignite our sense of caring and concern, stepping down two or three notches to take our place, humbly, in the vast scheme of nature. Fearing the immanent extinction of all ninety species of whales in the world, the International Whaling Commission, in 1986, passed a moratorium on hunting whales in international waters. Whales continue to die.

The World Wildlife Fund, in its 2020 Living Planet Report, emphasized that in less than fifty years, from 1970 to 2016, hunting, fishing, and logging had driven a shocking two-thirds of the world's wildlife population into extinction. Over that same period, populations of mammals, birds, fish, amphibians, and reptiles plummeted by an alarming 68 percent.

If human beings had set out with a deliberate plan to destroy nature, they could not have worked more effectively. How bizarre to point to the efficiencies of killing, as if a war against nature had been going on in earnest for some time and, over the ages, had achieved a perverse perfection.

One could very well believe it to be the case: By 1850, Grey whales had been hunted to near extinction. Five out of thirteen species of whales appear on the list of endangered species, the Right whale nearly gone. The North Atlantic Right whale and the orcas that inhabit the Salish Sea, are critically endangered. The humpback and other types of orcas, have at least been trying to return to life, on account of the international moratorium on whale hunting. While it is hard to gauge the entire population of the many species of whales, the International Whaling Commission estimates that prior to the onslaught of commercial whaling, Blue whales were what the IWC termed as "abundant," in every one of the four major oceans. Whatever their number might have been—and by all accounts it was more than "abundant"—a majority of those thirteen species now face extinction.

Between 1868 and 1971, the IWC reports that—and they present their findings with what they call "a high level of confidence"—commercial whalers killed an astonishing 382,595 Blue whales, which means that, on average, whalers killed ten Blues every day, over an entire century! Such horrific killing must be seen as beyond relentless, something deserving of the animal equivalent of genocide. For such killing disregards morality, ethics, and all concern for sentient beings, far beyond logic and language. Such killing loses sight of the suffering that whales undergo as they struggle to keep alive after being hit with a cannon-fired harpoon, sometimes three, or four, or more times. What can we call killing of animals on such a grand scale? We might settle on *theriocide*, a word that does not appear, even in the second edition of the OED, but which derives from the ancient Greek word, *therio,* which means "beast" or "animal." In our anger and condemnation, we now have the need to name and define.

Nonetheless, and even without a proper word to describe their havoc, such killers of nature—and by association human nature—must be brought to justice, for with their killing, they have destroyed the balance of life, not just for the creatures in the oceans, but for those that live on and in the ground, and those birds that build their nests in the tops of the most ancient trees.

One must sound that sentence out loud again. Those outlaws killed without constraint and, while *we* did not participate, we must still hang our heads in collective shame and guilt, and keep them bowed for the havoc that has taken place. The scale of killing, the devastation, the utter madness exists beyond human comprehension, for it is, indeed, inhuman. Norway now kills more whales than any other country, outdoing the determined Japanese, killing close to 600 in 2022, alone, and, according to the IWC, since the 1986 global moratorium, and in defiance of the act, has killed some 15,000 whales. Japan, Norway, and Iceland do not recognize the authority of the moratorium.

Melville chose well, for whales test the limits of reason and the imagination, and stretch our sense of what is possible. To realize that they are mammals means to see them as warm-blooded, as kin. Still, human beings treat them as a travesty. Whales must be protected, even though they are much too large, magnificent, and beautiful to be an oversight. But they obviously need bodyguards, and we must find the means to intercede, which means that we must keep our hands off them. But, if the largest of creatures need protection, we must wonder about the chipmunk, the beaver, and the squirrel tree frog, which is barely noticeable, as it changes color to avoid death.

Over the course of the nineteenth century, this country killed 500,000 Blues, which prompts the question, once again, why, and to what end? What does such perversion say about our legacy? Even if those creatures were not mammals or not majestic and colossal, we must confront the human drive to eradicate life so thoroughly and in such barbaric ways. What is it in the whale that warps our behavior so dramatically? Why do we find it so essential to eliminate majesty in such grotesque numbers and with such ferocity? Must we kill until the entire ninety species of whales, dolphins, and porpoises have gone extinct? To make the case more immediate and tragic, we must consider that those extraordinary creatures are the largest animals, outside of dinosaurs, known to have taken up life on this Earth. Their measurements stagger the imagination.

The Antarctic Blue whale is the largest animal ever to have lived, an astonishing 100 feet long, weighing 200 tons—400,000 pounds—with a lifespan of some eighty to ninety years. Their tongues, alone—nearly impossible to imagine—can weigh as much as an elephant, 5,400 pounds, while their hearts—the largest of any creatures on the planet—weighing 2,000 pounds, beat once every ten seconds, so loud the thumping can be heard with sonar two miles away. Such a behemoth must consume over 40,000,000 tiny shrimp, or krill, roughly 8,000 pounds of those tiny creatures every day. So powerful are they that some whalers steered clear of them. A leviathan in the truest sense, the Blue is a mythical creature of biblical proportions and beyond, too powerful to commodify.

Blues can remain under water for an entire hour, so that, even with its gargantuan proportions, few people ever see them. When the Blue whale does breach, air and water fly from the two blowholes at the top of its head to a height of some thirty feet. That such a miracle of nature would ever be hounded, tortured, and slaughtered is a crime of the highest order. And yet, there is the killing:

Since 1966, Blues have held a secure place on the list of Endangered Species.

Even worse is that many of them died just for the sheer, so-called sport of killing, or for the thrill of killing something spectacular and huge. It is an impoverished, perverse game—the thrill of throwing enough harpoons into a sentient being until it dies, sometimes seeing it suffer for one or two hours, one that is difficult, if not impossible, to understand. Should a person even understand the cold-blooded murder of warm-blooded mammals? Perhaps taking a life so close to the heart of Creation feels like a most victorious, powerful act, one that rivals the might of God, a sordid reversal of the beginning of life, itself. Such a primal act seems to make killers feel like kings.

Long after ships were moved by the wind and killing was carried out by hand, the hunt for whales increased. On the newly mechanized, technologized, and thus more efficient death ships, hunting and killing were done with radar, sonar, cannons, high-powered explosives called "whale bombs," night-vision scopes, and electronic tracking devices able to locate whales far beneath the surface, in any weather, and at any time of the day or night. Like all else in the mechanized and thus modernized century, killing was done more swiftly and efficiently. Even against those instruments of death, two hundred tons of Blue whale did not give up life without a ferocious fight.

Moby Dick is a bull Sperm whale, with eighteen to twenty-six teeth on each side of its lower jaw, each tooth weighing more than two pounds! Like cracking a rockfish or a crab, Moby Dick removed Ahab's leg in a single bite. In what is, perhaps, the only act of disgust possible for a whale, a split second after it "reaped away" Ahab's leg, Moby Dick spit it out. A whale can not only feel revenge, but can also make known its reactions.

In our fatigue and confusion, we might ask, what is the loss of a single sparrow, or one pigeon, more or less? Notice, we have no way of asking the sparrow or pigeon how it feels about giving up its one and only life; we cannot question the Fir what it derives from having the Spotted Owl nest in its uppermost branches. How can we make it evident, apparent, and above all else, obvious, that life is sacrosanct, and that its miracle exists outside of and in spite of numbers? We must not capitulate: Not one sparrow or passenger pigeon can be sentenced to death, for each creature is a critical thread in the warp and weft of nature.

The International Union for the Conservation of Nature lists 42,100 species threatened with extinction, twenty-eight percent of the population. 1,300 more have been deemed critically endangered and nearly extinct. The world either grows in complexity and wonder, or it shrinks, simplifies, ossifies, desiccates, and dies. The expansion of a capital economy, nature's enemy, must kill off creatures in ever-increasing numbers. If the animals had their way, they might place homo sapiens on a list of the most dangerous.

Melville saw the lust that was building for this new land-locked oil, the murky, slick, and gooey stuff that entrepreneurs no longer skimmed off the surface of rivers, or dug up underground, using ever more powerful machinery, or with dynamite and hydraulic pressure, forcing it, with great violence, to erupt from deep within the bowels of the Earth. The Drake Well, in Pennsylvania, bored out in 1859, reached a depth of some 69 feet. By 1901, just two years following the death of Melville, oil gushed from 1,021 feet underground at Spindletop. By 1948, wells were being drilled to a depth of 3,500 feet and, sixty years later, by 2008, with hydraulic fracturing, coupled with over 1,000 chemicals in a deadly concoction, the average well reached 6,000 or more feet.

The depth of those wells, from a mere seventy feet, in the middle of the nineteenth century, to those in the middle of the twentieth century, which reached over a mile below ground, does more than reveal the fact that oil was harder and harder to find, and entrepreneurs had to dig deeper to get at it. It reflects a ramped-up aggression, a rage for oil that required new and powerful machinery and new techniques for getting more of it and much faster, no matter how great the cost to living things. Nothing could stop those newly minted Ahabs from going after the big kill, no matter the level or fragility of the underground water table, or the possibility of polluting aquifers, or how such radical drilling might then poison animals. The oil we extract today began decomposing in the Mesozoic age, some two hundred and fifty to seventy million years ago: Like blatant criminals, corporations have broken into the Earth, stolen its riches, and claimed innocence. Undoing the Earth's very own history, they hauled up, burned up, and messed up all of life.

Melville also saw the inevitable dismantling of the natural world, which began with whales, and then with rivers and fish, with trees and its tiny inhabitants, and finally with deeply sequestered, underground oil. And there it was, both for the finding and the taking, that most precious gift called petroleum—"rock oil"—fueling first the appetites of con artists, then the machinery of industry, that is to say, enflaming the fiery heart of capitalism, itself.

What is the nature of that miraculous substance? Why do so many everyday products derive from petroleum, or rely so heavily on it, beginning, obviously, with all things plastic, but also lipstick, fertilizer, upholstery, golf balls, tennis balls, hand lotion, tooth paste, heart valves, food preservatives, trash bags, the roads people drive on, the tires that roll on those roads, critical medicines and their containers, and hundreds and hundreds of other common household items, including computers.

Did those with money exploit oil so that they might take control of the natural world, making the idea more certain with a ramped-up vengeance, a level of exploitation that has passed well beyond any natural limit? Are we now in the same fix as Ishmael, refusing or unable to recognize, let alone acknowledge, our condition? Do we continue yapping while drowning? Our own ship of state does, indeed, seem to have broken apart, shattered beyond recognition, setting us adrift, leaving us hoping to be rescued by some passing Good Samaritan.

We might find an answer, of sorts, to our own plight, in Chapter XXV, "Postscript," a startling interruption in a long tale of hunting and killing that comes, not after the conclusion to the story, where readers would normally find it, but following page 160, in a book of over 800 pages. We wonder, then, Postscript to what? Have we missed Melville's conclusion, and so close to its beginning? Has the point of the narrative, like a tide that rises ever so gradually, so imperceptibly, taken place without our noticing?

The Postscript serves as Ishmael's own declaration, his Manifesto within a Manifesto, in which he attempted to establish his own bona fides, through describing the place of whale oil in the history of various oils, as well as underscoring the immediately previous chapters, in which he bragged that "a whale ship was my Yale College and my Harvard University." It is a moment, perhaps, when Ishmael moves off-script— entering a true post-script—where, released from the narrative of the Pequod and the episodes of the bible, he feels free enough to free-associate about human nature as well as his own nature.

Ishmael has been speaking/narrating for over one-hundred fifty pages, and it is time, he realizes, to assert that he knows what he is talking about here, in a kind of instant memoir of what a life squandered looks like—at least aboard a whaling vessel—perhaps one of the most poignant and confessional chapters in a novel driven both by certainty and the arrogance of a rage ramped up to a seething outrage. By fracturing the narrative with a post-script, Ishmael, the person who we have been asked to trust, having abandoned his religious script, can now improvise as his own self, take action as a person. For the moment, he is the only person alive.

As we begin to see him so exposed and vulnerable, we are inclined to call him something other than Ishmael. To keep believing in him as his biblical impersonation puts our belief in his rescue in doubt, for the biblical Ishmael is saved in the desert by an angel, who brings something of which our narrator needs not one more drop: water. Aboard the rescue ship Rachel, he will be the biblical Ishmael no more, but rather whoever he is or chooses to be.

In a rage worthy of Ahab, a rage that sears the wound of daily living, Ishmael insists that whaling is a degraded pursuit that reveals just how debased contemporary life had become. An inspirited, luxurious life was now dependent on oil, not simply to keep those machines that were beginning to dominate daily life in full spin, but to keep them turning over and over at top speed.

As evidence, Ishmael points out, we ought to notice that it is in religion where we find the highest respect for oil, reserved for the anointing of priests and other holies: Both *mashiach* (messiah) and *christos* (Christ) translate as "the anointed one." Christ's own anointing, mentioned in all four gospels, was carried out with oil and a rare, fragrant flower called the spikenard. Ishmael laments that, from its elevated use, oil has fallen to the mundane act of dressing salads. On May 6, 2023, King Charles became the first royal to be anointed without the addition of ambergris. He wanted his coronation to be "animal-cruelty free."

Ishmael is urging us to understand something deeply significant, that the arrogation of oil, its appropriation for the new machine age, has meant a shift in the locus of worship from Church to factory, from Savior to sales counter and, as Henry Adams predicted, from supplicants who once honored the Blessed Virgin, to the duped who now genuflect at the feet of the Dynamo. Ishmael concludes with a bit of irony, or perhaps something closer to a display of rough humor: "Certain I am, however, that a king's head is solemnly oiled at his coronation, even as a head of salad. Can it be, though, that they anoint it with a view of making its interior run well, as they anoint machinery?" It is a poignant observation, a view of contemporary life that has denied the sacred.

As if he were seeing the truth for the first time, Ishmael records the rise and decline of oil, from its power to anoint to its ability to debase and degrade, in line with the loss of meaning in the very act of living: "But the only thing to be considered here, is this—what kind of oil is used at coronations? Certainly, it cannot be olive oil, nor macassar oil, nor castor oil, nor bear oil, nor train oil, nor cod-liver oil. What then can it possibly be, but sperm oil in its unmanufactured, unpolluted state, the sweetest of all oils? Think of that, ye loyal Britons! We whale men supply your kings and queens with coronation stuff!"

Melville, the slightly mad brooder, gives us more than just the sacred ritual of anointing that has been downgraded to little more than dressing on a salad, or the greasing of a machine. Through the loss of the holy, of the sacred, of belief and ritual, we get a glimpse of the demise of the well-being and vigor of a society, of the degradation of life, itself. Can a sense of wonder ever be recovered? The images seem to close off the possibility.

Through that one element, oil, Melville set the highest ritual of religion against the lowest level of the mechanical, as if he saw what Henry Adams realized a bit later, that the machine had already usurped the holy; that to keep the machinery of commerce running efficiently would demand endless barrels of oil; and that petroleum would be the anointing oil of the new economy. For Melville, on the grandest scale and widest range, in a mockery of the religious, oil debased all that it touched.

As a preview of the new world, Melville has Ishmael explain how banal that most precious, most holy substance had become. The age of the machine demolished the real and created its own distorted, nearly perverted brand of religious fascination.

Throughout the book, Melville makes plain his disgust of the new machinic age and its ugly aftermath, embodied in the being and behavior of Ahab, whose biblical lineage, in 1Kings: 16, aligns him with the wicked king who marries Jezebel, a devotee of the Canaanite demon Baal. Her corrupting influence on religion has infected this mad sea-captain. It is a theme picked up by that other biblical character, also possessed of a single name, Ishmael, in whom the religious connection remains and which, at the end, becomes accentuated. For he opens the narrative by confessing a fault and a desire, that because he found "nothing particular to interest me on shore," he set out for the sea. He had hoped to do better; he had needed to feel better; he had wanted to find something better. Ishmael needed some cure-all, but, alas, he had only himself.

In the beginning Ishmael could not heal himself, for he was like a teetering top, off kilter, slightly or moderately dyspeptic, even somewhat splenetic, and while he was prone to fits of ill-temperament, his rage has been cooled, at least for the moment, by treading water, neck-deep and in the middle of the ice-cold Atlantic— there is a tempering in his telling. He is saving himself by recounting his story, by recollecting, confessing, and making himself lighter, and in that process, undergoing a transformation.

Ishmael—a biblical character reimagined as an unintentional martyr, and then reconceptualized as fictional hero—comes to understand, during the course of his telling, what actually happened on his doomed voyage, and he has limited time to tell it, and no one around to corroborate the details, but also no one to contradict them. He knows someone is listening, but knows not who. But he is never without a witness, for when he speaks, as we know, "God Hears." We have faith that this person will tell us the truth—or, at least, his truth. Ishmael watches the Pequod as it breaks into tiny pieces, spinning around and around as it gets sucked, slowly, beneath the surface of the ocean. At a much deeper level and over the course of 800 pages, he tells us what actually fell apart and got sucked into its watery grave.

Ishmael signed on board because he had his fill of moping about on land. He craved adventure, needing to re-animate his life. Sick at heart, he did more than sign on to the Pequod. He left the land and its woeful ways, for the adventure of the voyage. Like Melville, he became disillusioned by so much killing. And so, he called his own fate into being. Why did it all go so wrong, a question he tried to get at by understanding the person who took command over his life, a man with the title of a mountebank, "Captain."

And so, as Ishmael narrates his doomed voyage, ridding himself of guilt, he has no choice but to fall back on his assumed character, on his biblical shadow-self, knowing that as an orphan and an exile, he ought to be saved by a miracle. In the middle of the ocean, Ishmael floats and bobs, a pale imitation of Moby Dick, surrounded by bits of his mother ship, wondering why this has happened, all the while knowing that, once again, because of his name and his biblical shadow of a self, he will be saved. Indeed, he will be plucked out of the sea by the Rachel, a ship named for a woman in the bible who is desperate to bear a child, and who confronts her husband, Jacob: "Give me a child or I will die." Given the chance, Rachel would embrace Ishmael as her own. Women go nearly missing in *Moby Dick*, natality and nurture replaced by drama and death. The Ur-mother, not Rachel but the Earth, itself, has been ravaged: Natality is absent from the telling. Nothing is born, but a tremendous amount dies. While the Pequod is an emblem of death, here at the end of the telling, the Rachel suggests birth and even rebirth, the promise of a new beginning, the restoration of nurture and care.

Aboard the Pequod, the outcast Ishmael began, slowly, to resemble in temperament his monster of a boss, saved, in the end, by his own broader vision and understanding, capped or sealed by entwining fingers with his mates. He can articulate for us the deep sense of bully power, not as it informed the person of Ahab, but in the authority that has been conferred on Ahab by his rank as Captain. A captain gives commands and he commands respect; underlings must obey. The captain plots the course; the crew, of course, must agree with the commander's plan. Ishmael has no title, but must try to lead through language, vision, and his sense of humanity, through the insistence conferred on him by the truth. And, thus, his need to establish the right to narrate—aligning his name with his essence—bring me to an animate life, and do it now, before it is too late: "Call me Ishmael."

Without *authority*—cognate with *author*—he cannot narrate—no one can. Ishmael, in particular, must get hold of such authority, for he is in a most confounding circumstance, of fluency and erasure, of currency and erosion, making sense while adrift, in the vastness of the ocean, up to his neck and a bit higher, without another living being in sight. Everything familiar has disappeared deep under water, having returned to the beginning of all beginnings.

And this is part of what changes during the course of the narrative, for Ishmael's opening gambit—"Call me Ishmael"—has taken on meaning, a most poignant plea: Name me and activate me. Grant me my name, and you grant me meaning, a script of significance. And so, take me seriously as the biblical figure that I feel closest to, in order to provide shape/hope in my own life. Believe in me and you aid in rescuing me. Agree to name me and you grant me life. Two levels of rescue touch on the narrator: The reader keeps Ishmael's spirit alive by granting him his identity, while the Rachel will pluck him from the water granting him his rebirth into a new and enlightened life.

All the while, aboard this vicarious or hallucinatory voyage, the listener gets blown into a new and alarming category, and into a time when countless Ahabs will come to an abundant and thoroughly frightening life on land—into a time in which nothing can stop the ship of state, nothing can startle, not even the holy insistence of a whale. For, under the full sail of Ishmael's narrative, the reader continues sallying forth, without a clear destination, into a time under the control of those newly anointed Captains of Industry, multi-millionaires, billionaires, and those most-recent sports of capitalism, the centi-billionaires. The amount of havoc that they can wreak reaches beyond the unimaginable.

For the country arrived, much too quickly, far too abruptly, at an unbelievable level of destruction in which whales die in untold numbers, not by harpoon or lance, but from a deadly by-product of petroleum, billions of tiny plastic pellets called "nurdles," an estimated 250,000 tons of them ending up each year in the oceans. In the ocean, pellets move and bob about, reflecting light, as facsimiles of real food—the deadliest of lures, which whales instinctively devour and from which they slowly die.

In May 2022, a Cuvier's Beaked Whale beached itself off the Island of Rhodes, intact to the eye but dead to the world. An autopsy revealed that over thirty pounds of those nurdles were lodged in its stomach and blocking its organs. Marine biologists concluded that the whale "had died a painful death." The Natural History Museum estimates that Beluga whales in the Arctic, on account of the microplastics in the fish they eat, consume an average 145,000 bits of plastic in a single year, slowly and unwittingly killing themselves. Who is responsible for these strange deaths, and what should be the punishment?

Is there an indictable "we," a band of renegades who have decimated the Earth? Or, should the fault reside mainly, especially for us contemporaries, with those 100 petrochemical corporations responsible for over 70 percent of the world's greenhouse gases? In the end, of course, such questions matter, but matter less and less as life fast fades, as emphasis shifts from culprit to solution. Every single plank, nail, and board of the Pequod has been shattered, undone and unmoored on account of a madman's obsession. The sea has reclaimed all its crewmembers, except, of course, for one. None of those thirty-odd men will ever undergo a burial, or ever know of ceremony. We cannot allow this to be another furious tale signifying nothing. At the very least, it tells us that killing will ultimately destroy the killers.

When the Rachel came upon the Pequod early in the narrative, its Captain, someone named Gardiner, was so desperate for help that he took the drastic step of boarding the Pequod: Captain confronting Captain. Before Gardiner had a chance to speak, Ahab revealed his obsession: "Hast seen the white whale?" Ignoring the question, Gardiner begs him to help find his son, lost overboard in a whaling boat, days earlier, in the hunt for Moby Dick. Somewhere, Gardiner tells the madman, he may be adrift, in the vastness of the sea, struggling to hang on to his life.

Ahab listens and immediately, stoutly refuses. He is on his own mission, to find and kill that hunk of evil masquerading in white, and his obsession excludes the prospect of helping others, and certainly not his competition, this man called Gardiner. That Gardiner is also pursuing Moby Dick only spurs Ahab into resuming, with immediate speed, his insistent killing. Nothing can stand in his way; nothing can slow him down or stop him, and certainly not a plea to play the Good Samaritan.

The arrival of the Rachel, with Ishmael floating "for almost one whole day and night," obviously rules out the possibility that, out of retaliation, Gardiner might not pluck our friend from the sea. Gardiner acts, after all, as the Good Samaritan. When the Rachel rescues Ishmael, "on the second day," events once again underscore a biblical narrative, with Ishmael becoming Gardiner's adopted son, a surrogate for his own son. In the final sentence of the book, Ishmael says: "It was the devious-cruising 'Rachel,' that in her retracing search after her missing children, only found another orphan."

Captain Gardiner makes it possible for Ishmael to assume an identity, no longer as an orphan out of the

bible, but as a person plucked out of the cold and indifferent, amniotic waters, hoisted aboard the Rachel, where
he can assume his new identity. The good ship Rachel
will have delivered a child from drowning, one who has
floundered in the sea for two days and nights, surrounded
by sharks that "glided by as if with padlocks on their
mouths." Gardiner will have rescued the person critical
to broadcasting the truth after the telling is finished, an
Ancient Mariner doomed to retailing his tale. Ishmael
sounds the lone voice in the Epilogue, toned down but
poignant: "And I am escaped alone to tell thee."

The "end" becomes an "ending," a never-ending tale,
as the story lurches into its own dislocation from biblical narrative, and sails off into a new, fully resuscitated
narrative, full-sail in our own imaginations. Manifestos
typically do not end, but get subsumed by the reader. The
last line of the *Manifesto of Futurism* screams of power
forever alive and forever barely in reach: "Lift up your
heads! Even on the summit of the world, once again we
hurl defiance to the stars!" The last line of the *Communist
Manifesto* is a call to awaken and take charge: "Working
men of all countries, unite!"

As readers, we have assumed the role of a dry-land
version of Ishmael, cast adrift in our own wondering.
Melville makes us ponder, then, how the story will end,
and what will happen to that life-line, Ishmael. Where
will he go? What can he do? Who does he know? He will
keep telling but who will keep listening? Will we miss

him? And we must take heed, for his lessons must be made manifest by us, for we, too, belong to the generation of sole survivors.

In the beginning, Ishmael believed in the malevolence of the whale and in its demise, which is to say, he believed in Ahab, and he believed only in the half-hearted way that a man cast down with spleen could believe. Over the course of the voyage, Ishmael did not radically change. Rather, he began to live more and more into the name that he selected and the one that we, as accomplices, in our collusion, agreed to give him. Granting Ishmael his life, the reader must be the first to rescue him. At the instant he meets us, he has been moved to unfold the tale of hate on the voyage, the rage that fueled it, and the price that the entire crew paid for such excess. We listen to an extended tale from a man who has seen far too much hatred and killing and who can take no more, and so has cast off his life, and repented, all of it in preparation for the grand rescue.

As listeners, we have helped Ishmael to remain above water and to stay alive, enabling him to tell us of his slow swoon under the spell of a madman: "I, Ishmael, was one of that crew; my shouts had gone up with the rest; my oath had been welded with theirs; and stronger I shouted, and more did I hammer and clinch my oath, because of the dread in my soul. A wild, mystical, sympathetical feeling was in me; Ahab's quenchless feud seemed mine. With greedy ears I learned the history of that murderous monster against whom I and all the others had taken our oaths of violence and revenge."

We come to realize that life, itself, did not seem right to Ishmael, and then something snapped, pulling this strange and estranged personality, more and more, into his biblical name, as he began to take on a conscience, revealed, once again, in his narration. And thus, immediately, he asks for a name, and by his decision, we both have been granted a bit of hope. We, too, have a chance to change: Some higher or greater authority—name it what you will, conscience, morals, ethics, a calling, religion, or even God—hovers and hears, and overhears. Ishmael invites us back to a prior beginning, a chance to play Adam.

While Ishmael took hold of Ahab's rage and ingested it, he came, in time, to regurgitate it all. And we must learn from that conversion. We must try to turn our own massive, slow-moving, and monumentally heavy ship of state around. We must try, with all our might, to rescue this orphaned planet as well as our own orphaned selves, our own deprived and belittled beings. Call us all Ishmaels: Hear our sad tale, as sole survivors, you higher powers, and be kind.

Such is Melville's desire. But it is also Ishmael's, as he has learned his lessons through the master and maestro of the blistering art of rage. We could not refuse Ishmael's initial plea or request, because by agreeing to call him Ishmael, we became responsible for bringing that estranged literary noun into a fleshier and much more believable verb, and by listening to his tale, we took responsibility for keeping him alive. And so, we agreed to call him Ishmael, which means that we must hear him out and take his word seriously.

By some downright clever literary maneuvering, we have become responsible for keeping our new acquaintance afloat and for attending to what he has to say. If we keep turning pages, Ishmael can maintain his breath. If we listen, we also act. He is the truth situated within the insistence of the Manifesto. He is filled with a rage that has been awakened but which has also been curtailed, refined, and thus elevated. He now has know-how and knowledge; he has seen killing and destruction firsthand. He is as close as possible to that ennobled rage which inspirits the classical rhetor, and thus the charge that enables the *Iliad* to set sail.

We must do more than listen: We must learn to hear, and to notice. Moreover, we must act. We must begin to speak as if we, too, were all Ishmael-like figures, speaking while near-drowning, and knowing that some greater power overhears. We must decide how to act and what to do. Nothing less than the future of the planet is at stake. This is especially so since Melville writes so sparingly of the future, as if he could not believe in such a figment of language. While *Moby Dick* is so much about obsession, arrogance, and revenge, driven by rage—or carried along by that emotion—and exasperated and intensified by an active and powerful pull into the future, Melville hardly if ever invokes the future tense. In a Manifesto, while the argument implies a future, or near future, action is always planted in the present, in the moment, activated by commands: "Lift up your heads! Hurl defiance to the stars!"

Melville's sea story takes place, not only with little or no mention of the future, but as if there were no tense and no destination whatsoever, as if the men on the *Pequod* simply and only experience time by carving notches into a piece of ivory, or by recalling sightings of some familiar whale. Rage has the power to pull a person out of time, to take up life deep inside that charged emotion, and so obliterating the future, making acts of killing easier, close to a figment, a mere looming.

The vastness of the sea creates the illusion of being becalmed forever, of being held fast, even with a ship under full sail: Time simply stalls. Such stillness, or "in-placeness" resembles a serene religious state, everything becalmed, all attention fastened on God. The future collapses onto the present, the past evaporates— unless, like Ahab, a person has but a singular thought and with it, and on account of it, a drive that seeks revenge. The surround of watery nothingness (or of everything) induces a misguided clarity, as if one were being offered a glimpse of the beginning before the beginning, itself. Thus, Ahab finds himself in charge of everything he sees, and all that he thinks he sees.

Whatever the existential case, a sense of the movement of time is critical, not solely for the act of thinking, but for thinking, and thus for plotting and scheming or, most to the point here, for planting the seed of mutiny, of overturning the status-quo. A stillness out of time may support meditation, but it will not do for the radical activities of scheming and acting. Every report on climate change situates the crisis (and the solution) within time—glaciers melting faster than scientists had predicted; people having less time to reduce greenhouse gases to near zero; civilization living in a new era called the Anthropocene; and on and on.

In the telos of the Earth, time is running out; or, rather, we are out of time. It is time to act. Surely, out there, somewhere, Captain so-and-so, and his ship, the Good Samaritan, must be under full steam, on course to save us. But that is our undoing: We are orphans, and we are dependant. Our mother lies dying, calling out for our help, and the disfiguration leaves us flummoxed—even ashamed. She needs us, now, to stanch the flow of blood, to resuscitate and restore her health, and we have forgotten first- and even second-aid, as well as CPR. The good ship Rachel arrives on a wave of hope and a crest of the future. We stare into the horizon and think we make out the outline of a ship.

In the entirety of *Moby Dick*, Melville provides but a vague sense of the future, with a single use of the word *tomorrow*, in the penultimate chapter, titled "The

THE MANIFESTO OF HERMAN MELVILLE

Chase—Second Day." Here is Ahab as seer, his warning to the crew told through the erratic behavior of the
whale: "Believe ye, men, in the things called omens?
Then laugh aloud, and cry encore! For ere they drown,
drowning things will twice rise to the surface; then rise
again, to sink for evermore. So, with Moby Dick—two
days he's floated—to-morrow will be the third. Aye, men,
he'll rise once more—but only to spout his last! D'ye feel
brave men, brave?" How odd that Ahab, dispossessed of
the mystical and magical, predicts the outcome on that
magical day, number three. Instead of the renewal of the
future, tomorrow will spell death for the whale.

One final chapter remains, CXXXV, "The Chase, The
Third Day." We have arrived at the end of the novel, the
end of the voyage, as well as the end of the telling, as
Ahab puts it, on day three. The last paragraph signals
both a ferocious ending of the hunt for the Apparition
and a beginning that is no beginning, a single sentence,
crafted mostly of monosyllables, loping forward on easy
rhythms, testing our tolerance for alliteration, all the
while reeking of the certainty of death: "Now small fowls
flew screaming over the yet yawning gulf; a sullen white
surf beat against its steep sides; then all collapsed; and the
great shroud of the sea rolled on as it rolled five thousand
years ago."

It is a death scene, a macabre one, with small birds
that no longer sing, but perhaps frightened by the disso-
nance of disorder, can merely scream; a surf humanized

and suddenly sullen; and the sea, where animate life began, transformed into a death shroud, because so much of life has been entombed there, the indifference of nature revealed in the sea rolling on, "as it rolled five thousand years ago."

In the concluding sentence, not a single person is present, only the natural world described by the human, in its "screaming," "yawning," or in its turning toward the "sullen," and death descending in imitation of "the great shroud of the sea": We are at the end of things, not on land, but in the unlaundered mysteries of the frightening infinitude of the sea—where sentient life began and both time and territory cease to be.

Melville writes here as if all human life had not just vanished, but that human activity had left no mark—akin to water continuously eroding and erasing—except in the most ferocious ways that people know—by destroying beauty and wonder and killing some of nature's most majestic creatures, so much of that destruction out of view, either in the deep woods or the deep ocean. Ishmael is an outcast twice over, once when he left the land for the sea, and later when he was jettisoned from the Pequod. And, as an ending also comes to describe us, we can either suffer as outcasts, Isolatoes—or we can come alive to regain our own humanness and ensure the liveliness of those remaining creatures. Under the domination of technology, we have become "transcendentally homeless," figments on the World-Wide-Web. We need to beat a path back home.

We human beings had our time and botched it badly. Oceans, thoroughly polluted, continue in the course they have taken for the past hundreds of thousands of years; and gulls, sick and dying, continue to sound their screech-high voices, here over a scene of utter ruination; over that sole-surviving human being; and over a whaling vessel that broke apart and slowly disappeared. Such a dismal scene says no to the future tense, no to even bare predictions. We need to look closely, for there is more than a single person needing rescue here, more than one person to be saved from drowning.

Out of a crew of some forty-four people—though in the last chapter Melville counts but thirty (the number of states in the Union at that moment)—under the control of one single-minded and mightily ferocious Captain, only Ishmael has brought us the details of the voyage and its conclusion. Bereft and in need of nurture, Ishmael relies on his painful and complicated biblical roots— he has pursued a narrative that ends with a miracle. Compared to the whale, Ishmael seems painfully awkward, desperately displaced, and if he were not so close to dying, we might say he is close to laughable.

Denied the prospect or the reality of a future, we begin to feel as if we, too, are close kin to Ishmael, marooned somewhere in the immensity of a wide-open, never-ending body of . . . water, or thought, or some techno-experiment. We wonder: Are we going anywhere? Is the story progressing? What does it mean, anymore, to utter words like "progress" or "progression?" I thought this was a Manifesto. What is manifest but death and destruction? Help, we need help. We need help now.

Enticed aboard the Pequod by Ishmael, and having sailed for a time, can we ever be certain that after undertaking an odyssey of such importance and confronting the horror of killing and destruction we will return to our home, our *oikos,* enlightened and made aware of the sacred? After putting the book down, can we say that we have been on a pilgrimage, our souls open and ablaze with meaning, our hearts recharged with a love for the endless miracle that is nature? At the end of this most magnificent voyage of language, have we entered into a new appreciation of everything that swims, scurries, and soars, and to all that we might include, in the divine retelling of time and of our own time, on this rock of meaning?

Melville's narrative cannot end with the death of that light-giving behemoth. It must end with the death of that other larger-than-life character, the source of madness, a creature with a soul so dark it absorbs all light, Ahab— only then might nature be vindicated. The death-ship must also perish. Both man and machine must sink from view, as nature has revolted, and we humans, responsible for dislodging the natural order, must pay the price. Under the grinding influence of a madman, there can be no other outcomes but failure and death. In the beginning of this tale, we saved Ishmael by naming him. In the end, that foundering beacon of hope returns the favor, helping to save us.

In the ending of *Moby Dick*, we must realize that the natural world has not so much triumphed—what could such a description actually mean, for those animals are not at war with us—but something has taken place that is closer to a word that Faulkner preferred, which is that humans have *endured*. Ahab has died. Moby Dick lives. Ishmael begins once more. The reader, too, has managed to struggle through. And the sea, as always, rolls on as it can only do, and has done, for the past five thousand years. The ocean is water and salt and changes from wave to wave, but in its shapeshifting, remains the same, covering some seventy percent of the planet. Human beings, nearly eight billion and counting, have planted themselves on but thirty percent of the planet, acting as if that tiny patch were infinite. In its slow dance, the sea offers but the illusion of change.

Can we really think of the future as some kind of wide-open, four-lane highway, free of potholes, tollbooths, and speed limits, offering a direct line to . . . who knows where—perhaps to wherever we choose to go, or wherever we imagine we want to go, or think we ought to go? Is Captain Ahab not tempting fate by riding on that future tense for so long—over three long years—taking along with him a cohort of unhappy, disgruntled, and hoodwinked sailors? Can anyone really believe in the promises of the future for more than just a moment? As savvy readers we know that after a time, disaster and defeat lurk around each bend or blind corner, ready to pounce and take us down, to disorient us even further.

How long can Melville keep this precarious end-game afloat? Well, as master of language, eight-hundred or more pages. Melville, an articulate upstart, has made it impossible to finish his book in one sitting, To read *Moby Dick* is thus to enter into time as slowly passing, and as time slowly running out; it is to know the future on pause, as we pick up the book again and again, eager to reach the conclusion. To read *Moby Dick* is, indeed, to surrender to a sea voyage, in which we are made to feel as if we are adrift in those many pages of slowly changing sentences in which the action seems to have been put on pause. We know that to reach the end is to find our own Moby Dick, that final page of blinding (or illuminating) whiteness, empty of meaning yet full of importance, blank page as mirror of our own image.

Melville has pulled off an astounding feat of storytelling, for he has given us a structure that splinters and shatters as thoroughly as the doomed whaling ship itself. The storyline periodically falls apart and has too many interior monologues, interruptions, outlandish descriptions, religious asides, and long lists, and yet it is marked by prose so bold, so magnificent that Melville's sentences continue to shape American fiction and its many experiments, with details that unfold and tumble, with soliloquies that surprisingly erupt, events that shock, and with destruction that passes for instruction. Every story, in the end, is a voyage into the unknown, into a future that is as real as it can possibly get, since in the end reality, too, comprised of the formalities and possibilities of language and grammar, of seeing what is there, and what ought to be there, and what we insist must be present, cleaves close to fiction.

In *Moby Dick*, language takes on life as a character, untethered and most complicated. After the Pequod has sunk and taken the entire crew with it, nothing remains but words and their skillful arrangement, or bizarre rearrangement, and the water-logged soul who utters them: It is all Ishmael—from his opening call for a name, to his announcement as a sole survivor, the telling is a single person. Instead of a resolution, Melville uses the half-drowning Ishmael to retrieve the past and the near-desperate Ishmael to recount its horrors. This is all we have—we have only a narrator floundering, waiting to be plucked from the sea. We have only the lesson that the seemingly victorious, now absent whale provides for us. And this Ishmael, burdened with authority, does not know if he has anything even loosely resembling a future. Finally, we have the ocean, in motion but motionless, in flux but forever the same.

The ghost-ship Rachel will retrieve Ishmael, the narration will come to a close, the Pequod and the committed reader both having reached an end, and both having been stopped but not becalmed together. Melville has not given us the traditional ending, which demands that loose ends get knit up tidily, that all the oddities and seeming miscues get satisfactorily explained, that all surprise identities get revealed, and perhaps most important of all, that the unsettled world finds itself restored and tucked back into its proper order. It is a time to exhale. Again, *Moby Dick* is not a novel, and definitely not its nineteenth-century facsimile, and there will be no sigh of relief, no exhalation, no feeling of completion or satisfaction.

At the conclusion of the book, then, we ask: What is this strange telling all about? How do we, as singular beings on land, fit into this massive unfolding of death on the ocean? What must we do? What can we do? We know that, after such a commitment of time and such an exposure to extreme hate and revenge, we have been called upon to do something, and to do something significant, difficult, even unpopular. Also, we must ask: What must we *not* do?

As Ishmael comes to the end of his tale, the emphasis turns to lost children overboard, exiled step-children in the wilderness, wounded sea creatures, orphans, the unwanted or the misunderstood—no matter the delineation, for they are all in need of succor, consolation, desperate to be rescued, embraced, identified and loved. In the end, we wonder if a future tense, or whatever remains of it, can still open its arms wide enough to

THE MANIFESTO OF HERMAN MELVILLE

embrace all of us, providing the illusion, at least, of a grand rescue? If not, if our future has been truncated, what must we do to pull our own selves, along with all those creatures, seen and unseen, from the brink of destruction? How to regain the hope of a future in a time without a belief in a future? How many creatures, through our behavior, have we orphaned?

To repeat, there seems to be no future in *Moby Dick*, and there really is no solid end, which is to say, no conclusion. The book comes to a close with an Epilogue, a lament, as we know, from the master of repentance, from that wanderer and outcast, Ishmael. Melville, again, provides no resolution, offers no conclusion, refuses past formulas—does not even say goodbye. Instead, we must provide our own solution for nature's survival: "Whether he can long endure so wide a chase and so remorseless a havoc; whether he must . . . like the last man, smoke his last pipe, and then himself evaporate in the final puff." Moby must live. We must live, and not evaporate like a puff of smoke. More than that, we must act and try to forge a future.

In the end of the entire end, that most protracted time of our dominance over almost everything, will have come to a weary close. People make their connection with the natural world, in great part, through their diet and regimen, in what they consume—animals, fish, fowl, vegetables, fruits, and plants, along with great helpings of the beautifully wild and the wholly majestic. Across the globe, over the centuries and eons—eight billion people and counting, at the moment—human beings have eaten the planet out of house and home and sucked it dry of its elements: We have killed far too much of its beauty. Our privileged status that allows us to consume such a huge portion of the animal kingdom suggests that we have no need for the future tense: Satisfaction is, of course, most intense in the present. The scientific solution to over-consuming: Through genetic engineering, gene splicing, CRSPR technology, cloning, and other insults to nature, technology has struggled to manufacture facsimiles of the real. Like the whales, we now ingest nurdles, without knowing it, which remain in our gut. We bite into apples that never rot, but that also never ripen. We eat salmon raised in concrete pools, that swim in endless circles, and must be injected with red dye number x and with antibiotics. They masquerade as salmon that have been hatched in streams, swim to the ocean, and return to their birthplace, there to lay eggs and die, but they do none of that. Instead, to repeat, they swim in lazy circles in their own waste.

Our voyage over, we have all arrived back at home port, returned to the place where we began. Unlike the salmon, we are not prepared to spawn and die. Indeed, we have had an adventure. Certain moments even thrilled us. But whether we are secure or not seems to be a question that no longer makes sense but which still deserves an answer. No one remains but Ishmael, and shortly he will be rescued: We are alone, on our own. Melville has abandoned us, nay, tricked us. The Epilogue is now its own Manifesto, for we have all become sons and daughters of Job, escaped and alone to tell the truth, Ancient Mariners all. We can make do with what we have; we need not dig and explore, exploit and destroy one day more. We are fine, for we know we are finite. But the feeling lingers and nags that, like Ishmael, we are all orphaned, a condition created by our own doing, having strangled and smothered to death our own mother so that we might assume the role of the all-powerful father.

If such a transformation of our own way of living is, indeed, destined to come to pass, then the entire family of animals that remains will not only somehow and miraculously survive us, they will also resume their own pacific beings and, absent our deliberate incursions, will all of them lie down, heave a sigh of relief and, with a knowing nod to each other, live in peace and walk in bliss—"the wolf and lamb, the leopard and kid, the calf with the lion and the fatling." And who is that innocent, the "little child" who will lead us? One can imagine that infant as a remodeling and recounting of us all, reborn or newborn, purged of anger, madness, and greed, newly burnished into innocence, like Ishmael in the vastness of his baptismal font, Oceanica, fully alive, christened with a new name, and buoyed by a new vision.

Here, in the "little child," one finds the image of happy *innocence*, in its most literal, basic and etymological meaning, a vision of creatures "incapable of causing harm." What a delightful thought, what a wonder for the building of civilization anew—total and absolute equality wherever we look. It is a consummation devoutly to work towards and most devoutly to be completed. If we are to save ourselves, equality of every kind must be made manifest. Time is fast running out.

Rachel, one of the most compassionate of mothers in the Bible, mourned for her two children, Ephraim and Benjamin, who were exiled by the Assyrians. One hundred years later, Jeremiah had a vision that Rachel continued to mourn for her two children. Fierce and serious, Rachel cares immensely, tempting us to believe that some Rachel or other may yet find us in our own exile, pluck us out of our misery, and place us back on land, where we belong. But when she does, or if she does, we must be ready: We must desire to believe with a fresh imagination, and act with a keen restraint. We must inhabit a different vision and thus a different world, which means we must go about the business of rescuing ourselves.

We learned a lot aboard the Pequod, in the vastness of the ocean where all things lose their edges, where every object becomes an oddity. In the infinity that is the ocean, we know that, even if we are able to see very little of it, the sea teems with life, from the smallest to the most oversized: On the ocean, we must proceed, much of the time, under full sail and blind faith, for navigation is difficult, as the ocean provides no precise directions, no seamarks, or details. The captain must plot the course and command with authority. He must be a man of faith, of sometimes blind faith, speaking with confidence and operating with trust—in himself, in the stars, and in his instruments. Relying on the exactness of degrees and seconds, he must determine precisely where his ship sits and where the dangers lurk.

Ishmael is nowhere, homeless, adrift, out of his element and neck-deep in water, confident he will be plucked from the sea. With no money in his purse, "and nothing particular to interest me on shore," he took off, some 133 chapters earlier, for whatever he might encounter on the wide-open sea. Now, finished with such drama, he is ready to return to land. At the moment, he flounders in an element without form, a medium that consumes anything dropped into it, devouring it wholesale, as if the sea were some perpetually wide-open maw. The sea accepts most willingly but returns most begrudgingly.

Ishmael has arrived at the end of his narration and the conclusion of the book, and thus we end our dependence on him and he on us, for he has been our captain on this extended voyage and, by keeping up with his palaver, we have kept him upright and above water. He is ready now to create a fresh start in a fresh world. His opening three words, "Call me Ishmael," which, at the outset, we might have mistaken for a command, now feel so much more like an impassioned appeal: After all my time wandering while aboard the Pequod and my need now to be rescued from the ocean, you might as well call me Ishmael, because that describes my plight better than any other name.

Ishmael bobs, as if in the most primal of waters, or in the outermost reaches of space; as if he were both adrift and aloft in the beginning of time, lost in any idea of time, ready to create, ready to start the narration of a new story, this one informed by the truth of his very last voyage and which will be the only story that can be told. But he is in need of a guide, some instrument to help him make it back home, for he finds himself at the moment, indeed, in the middle of nowhere. No matter where he drifts, he remains in that same middle of nowhere.

Melville has pulled off something most deliberate here, and also something extraordinary, something beyond the expectation of any novel, and perhaps beyond the expectation, as well, of any Manifesto: He has brought us, the reader, to the very end of this immense telling and at the very same moment, to the beginning of not just another story, but the suggestion of something fundamental and profound. Like Ishmael, we are faced with an echoing emptiness and in a strange arrangement, as if we were the only human being around and on solid ground. Melville, the writer with an immense reach, from the bible to the beginnings of Western literature, from primal urges to the more primal Leviathans, from incantations to commands, has placed us at the opening of a most colossal tale, at the beginning of the first story, of biblical creation, or more accurately, at the beginning of re-creation itself—Herman Melville, the poet of Beginnings, the maker of the Manifesto.

Perhaps it is time, then, to recognize that Ishmael has been radically transformed, from a killer with a harpoon to a speaker with a mouth, unafraid to use it, even knowing that God not only listens but overhears and judges each of his words and all of his sentences. Ishmael thus knows that he can never resort to an apology, an *apologos*, or literal turning away from what he has told us, for his word is not his alone. He has become someone who has learned and cares enough to become a surrogate creator or as someone who now holds onto the truth, a cosmic force pushing and urging us to act.

Hoping to be an orphan no more, Ishmael has been slowly transforming himself into an authority, the mother/father of our own rehabilitation. Ishmael hands over the tiring task of narration hundreds of thousands of words after Moby Dick has swum out of view. That might have been the dramatic end, but Ishmael, only nominally tied to the bible, has the task of beginning anew, of taking up the Incipit of Living. But what will be his name? And who will choose it? Who will deliver it?

From the Epilogue, as we know, it appears that Ishmael will be rescued, although the ship's captain,

Gardiner, to make the point again, owes nothing to anyone from the Pequod, having been rebuffed earlier by Ahab. But, after all that observing, and all that suffering and near drowning, Ishmael has earned a more meaningful and awakened way of living. He is without any instruments, divine or otherwise, to help him navigate his way back home, let alone that might aid him in re-inscribing the world. Nonetheless, the holy images suggest themselves, their divine shape prefigured in the previous chapter, in Ishmael's description of the Pequod, as it began to revolve faster and ever faster, a universe sinking beneath the surface, as if in a drain, turning and turning and finally disappearing.

Melville has inserted the ending inside the third and final day of the hunt to kill Moby Dick, on which day, Ishmael watches as "three men were tossed from out the rocky boat, and dropped astern." And then, following their fall, Ishmael finds himself pitched into the sea, alive but adrift, always in the middle of the ocean, more than just a bit out of control and, as always, alert to patterns and designs. At the dawning of day three, he will be rescued. Moby Dick, the holiest of creatures, will be hounded and hunted no longer. In its own outrage, that oversized character has rammed its mighty, forty-foot-long, 90,000-pound body, at thirty miles-per-hour, into the wooden hull of the Pequod, destroying everything, men and material, in a single blow, a grim foreshadowing, perhaps, of the destruction on land only possible with the most massive machinery.

In water up to his neck, Ishmael watches his former home, the wooden ship, as floating *oikos*, break into countless pieces and, as it sinks slowly out of view, marvels as the wreckage creates its own geometric and close-to-divine configuring—out of death, a rebirth: "And now, concentric circles seized the lone boat itself, and all its crew, and each floating oar, and every lance-pole, and spinning, animate and inanimate, all round and round in one vortex, carried the smallest chip of the *Pequod* out of sight."

Nothing more for us to see but the narrator, adrift in the open sea, clinging to a coffin that had been made for the outcast who became his good friend, Queequeg. He hangs on to his symbol of death turned lifesaver, talking and talking, the Pequod dangerously close, spinning furiously to its own demise, threatening to take him with it. Melville has torqued the narrative, which has been straight as the horizon, into a circle, his change in design the powerful image of the gyre, a whirling and powerful vortex. The image more accurately captures our lives as a spin on the axis of the Earth, re-imagined in a score of like movements: whirlwind, vortex, swirl, spiral, eddy, cyclone, twister, whirlpool, mandala, water spout, dust-devil, tumble-weed, tourbillon, revolution, revolver, whirling dervish, flying saucer, dynamo, infinity (a double-axis), and finally, the fateful Wheel under the command of Dame Fortuna.

The spiral informs Greek mythology, embodied in Charybdis, daughter of Poseidon who, cursed as a monster of the sea, ingested huge amounts of water and spat it back as a rapidly spinning whirlpool; and, in a favorite of Melville's, Okeanos, the Earth-encircling-river. Such forceful whirling and whirring, of course, marks the mighty dynamos that Henry Adams came upon, first with fascination and then with dread, initially in the Gallery of Machines, at the World's Columbia Exhibition, in Chicago, in 1893, and then, seven years later, in 1900, at the Paris Exposition, inside the ominously named Palace of Metallurgy and Mines.

In *Moby Dick*, all of that powerful, incessant turning, from vortex to whirlpool, from dust devil to dynamo, top and gyro, serves as mere rehearsal for its most memorable political invocation years later in Henry Adams. The image, indeed, begins in the heavens, in the great whirling high above people's heads, and ends in the ocean and beyond, beneath the waters, where so much killing has turned it into a "blood-dimmed tide," a mirroring that does not guarantee the reassurance of rebirth but leans hard in that direction.

The pull of Melville's particular vortex, created by the spin of sea water, is mighty and persistent, made more ferocious on account of salt, its suction grabbing hold of everything within range: "So floating on the margin of the ensuing scene, and in full sight of it, when the half-spent suction of the sunk ship reached me, I was then, but slowly, drawn towards the button-like black bubble at the axis of that slowly wheeling circle, like another Ixion I did revolve."

Around and around spins the narrator, leaving the bible for classical myth, turning now into Ixion, who was doomed to spin forever, on a wheel of fire. Ishmael is not Ixion; no one has agreed to call him that. He flounders, trading fire for water. He is spinning, dizzy—not thinking so clearly—the edge of the centrifuge moving ever closer and finally passing him by, allowing him to escape the mighty dynamo that threatens to suck him under. Ishmael's salvation, in that most critical, near final instant—for as long as this salvation lasts—appears as a miracle, with the power of an icon, or relic: A pine coffin suddenly leaps, whale-like, from beneath the sea. When Ishmael grabs hold of the deathbed, it becomes his life-preserver.

The coffin that had been built for Queequeg, intended for his final rest, ensures a new life for Ishmael, as if those two, so fearful of each other in the beginning of the voyage, had merged identities: "Call me Queequeg." Under water and of sight throughout the telling, the coffin that suddenly appears, as if sent from some unknown place or person, serves as a sign of deep and loving friendship, or even of love, from the drowned Queequeg: I give up my resting place, my bed, once again, for your benefit.

Whatever the case, Ishmael grabs it, and hangs on for dear life, recalling the scene when Ishmael awakens at the Spouter Inn, in bed with Queequeg's arm thrown around his neck. The scene, powerful and poignant, offers lessons in friendship, in coincidence, transformation, in divine intervention—in ordinary events spinning into the extraordinary.

Meanwhile, everything that once existed and had life gets sucked under the sea, pulled to its watery grave by the powerful gyre, the planets spinning high overhead reflected in the whirling waters of the deep ocean—again, as above, so below. Ishmael, too, has nearly gone under at this point, or at least that is how he sees it: "And so floating on the margin of the ensuing scene, and in full sight of it, when the half-spent suction of the sunk ship reached me, I was then, but slowly, drawn towards the closing vortex. When I reached it, it had subsided to a creamy pool." He is saved by yet another act of divine intervention, as the gyre runs out of spin, and all that was once dynamic slows to the last and lazy turn of the roulette wheel.

This man, who, as Melville says, has managed to exist on the margins of the action, has now been spared from being sucked into its center, floating at the edge of the whirling waters. He honors the miracle of his escape by narrating what he has witnessed during the entire voyage, by offering us his own dire warning, his memoir, to whomever will listen which, in the end, may only be to

God. Pitched from the Pequod, he has shed all identity, adrift as orphan, rescued by us with a name—"Call me Ishmael"—rescued once again by the Rachel.

Because he prefigured his life by borrowing from the bible, Ishmael knew that he must be rescued. He relied on his carefully chosen biblical destiny, one that he, himself, called into being: He gambled and he won. What he has to say at the end must now hold deep meaning for us all at this moment, in our own dilemma, in our own dread of being adrift up to our neck in despair, cast out of our *oikos*, our home, the Earth, itself: Like Ishmael, we hope and wait. Unlike Ishmael, we do not know if we will be rescued, and we certainly do not know how we will be rescued.

The great majority of people hope for a solution, praying that some bold rescue ship, from somewhere or anywhere, is steaming its way under full power, just to them and just for them. Far too many people hold on to the belief that, like a coffin turned life-preserver, science/technology will suddenly appear as a miracle, rescuing hordes of now desperate creatures, who have been orphaned, and who must now fend for themselves on this tattered planet. By now we know that every scientific fix results in a corrosive side-effect, sometimes more insidious than the problem, for which science must then find one more solution.

Our rescue does not appear to be in the offing—at least no time in the near future. And so, we must take a cue from that slowly submerging, slowly dying narrator. He will not go under for, in some ways, the idea of death, or of deep despair does not matter much at all for Ishmael, for he does not have the right state of mind for the end: He is too intent on thinking, too interested in pure cogitation and recollection, on trying to reorder things and, in the end, needing to repent far too much. Sadly enough, Ishmael seems to be cursed with faith, with the idea that there is still a chance at rectification, at the reality of rescue by a dint of resilience. He has relied on his biblical identity, but not for much longer.

We have reached the end of a very protracted tale and the explanation of how Ishmael got so immersed (literally) in such an extended narration in the first place and why after the voyage, and in the final phase of its recounting, that tale has become so critical. Ishmael feels he must risk his life to get the entire undertaking told, to unburden himself of what he now knows, to inform the world of what he has seen and learned and what we must take from his ragged and violent time at sea. He has been drifting for over eight hundred heavily inscribed pages to bring us the news, to riddle it out with precise detail and intense passion, at the peril of his own life.

Ishmael recognizes the end of this tragedy and he draws the curtain. Sounding a bit weary, the entire tale rushing so close to chaos, and needing to conclude, he utters for the second time in the narration a bare, three-word declaration: "The drama's done." The ending of

Moby Dick is chilling, haunting, downright frightening, somewhat enigmatic and puzzling. At the same time, it is fabulously invigorating and exciting.

In its demands, a Manifesto might touch on ideas that sound frightening, but the Manifesto must also pursue the possibilities of change, must offer at least a bit of hope. In its intent, the Manifesto must move people to excitement and propel them into action. Manifestos might be propounded deep inside a cave of anger, but they must be executed, always, in the open atmosphere of care, concern, and inclusion. Above all, and beyond all else, Manifestos are motivated by one desire—the liberation of all living things.

The choice here for Ishmael, post-rescue, is either to pursue more of the poignant—which means a life of continued wandering, wondering, and his eventual death— or a wild and hopeful plunge into creation, or re-creation, which always prompts a certain resistance. Ishmael may have to shed his name and take on a new identity that has less biblical insistence and pursue freedom through the power of his own being. If *Moby Dick* asks to be read as a Manifesto, the only one who can carry on and carry out the essential work, who can show us what to do and even how to do it, oddly, is an outcast whom we have come to know too well and who has handed over the task of saving the world from those bent on destroying it to his closest, most loyal ally, to those he has never met—to the reader.

Over the course of hundreds upon hundreds of pages, Ishmael has settled in as our intimate tattletale, the sole survivor of chaos who is used to translating events, playing a part, adopting the bible as his script. He is also the isolated and jettisoned one, the only who is able to pierce the action to gain understanding, heir to the abandoned, biblical Ishmael. And thus, we come to rely on his truth, for he utters the word most reliably. Melville, that scoundrel, has held our narrator-in-chief to the truth by nothing less than an act of divine eavesdropping, and thus has shaped our own hearing: We listen without judgment, for the truth remains irrevocably present.

The finality of what Melville needs to tell us, surprisingly, does not come in the final chapter, but rather in the Epilogue, a protracted statement set in a typeface designed for Rennaisance Papal Documents. Melville chooses as his epigraph a key moment from the bible, the delivery of the most poignant, painful truth retailed by a sole-surviving servant to Job, who lives in The Land of Uz, the "The Land of Words": "And I only am escaped alone to tell them." The phrases, "I only" and "escaped alone," lay bare the withering isolation and vulnerability of a survivor. He who sees and survives knows the blessing and curse of reporting the truth.

There is, thus, only one sentence the servant can utter out loud and only one response for having to deliver the truth of tragedy, for the price of his survival is that, as eye-witness, he must recount the unimaginable details of death and depravity. The servant's words reverberate with trepidation and horror: I, only, have escaped; forgive me for surviving. He who listens has the urge to kill. For to survive any horrific event raises basic questions of morality: Why did the messenger survive? What did he or she do to be elected? Was there capitulation with the enemy? The survivor must wonder, what do you think of me? Do others see me as suspect, a traitor to save my own skin? Ishmael, as sole survivor, has brought to us, the reader, our own horrible if not horrific, confounding, but devastating news.

As a sole survivor, Ishmael is perhaps not totally suspect, but he is also not totally enviable, not initially believable. He shoulders a burden. Those of us who have read *Moby Dick* in our own time also carry a burden, for there is much work to do; there is tremendous, near unbelievable devastation that must be repaired; and there is an overwhelming amount of rage that must be purged and replaced with something closer to outrage, followed by some less explosive emotion that can help effect change. Melville delivers the news, and it is close to awful. A great many people just might not like to hear it all.

William Blake depicts God with a compass in his hand, leaning over the broad expanse of chaos and inscribing a pattern, planning to create order out of nothing. God is, indeed, sometimes called the Divine Geometer. We must place a set of imaginary compasses over this, our contemporary, whirling chaos—over our gyration that is so dizzying and so destructive to life—and on the surface of that chaos inscribe a new plan and form, one that implicates us all, deeply and indelibly, in renewed inspiration and hope. Our ship of state, our Pequod, spins and turns, on the lip of the whirl, past the edge of being sucked under. Come to our senses, we must.

For a new order, or a new template of re-ordering, must build on a renewed shape to confront today's bewildering, nearly overwhelming version of free-form chaos and destruction of a world that has been gyrating out of all proportion, its centripetal force sucking every single person into its center, in some state of disorientation and dizziness, of semi-consciousness. Like children who shrug off gravity (and reality) by spinning around and around until dizziness takes over, far too many adults have shed control and, in a state of vertigo fall helplessly onto what is still most solid and familiar, a crash-landing on the firmness of terra firma, on land and not on water.

But, unlike those children at play, we have had our senses corrupted, and so, dizzy and still hugging our own selves to keep from flying apart, laughing out loud, we lose shape and split our sides. We are sad and we lament our condition and we suffer our pain. Bowing our heads in despair, we weep and weep some more. We have spun out of control. How reassuring if we could but fall back down and, like Ishmael, find our lifesaver—even a refitted coffin—and hang on for dear life.

Only human beings, out of care and concern, can set things back in place—if such a correction, any longer, is possible. We are well past the time for re-creation and rebirth, past expecting a tsunami of hope and a hallelujah of sheer exhilaration. Rachel has steamed its way past us and out of our line of sight. We must take charge, act, and respond to the wailing of the wolves, to the groaning of the bears, to the horror of the marooned penguins, and to the beached pilot whales, 477 of them in a single day, in January 2023, on the coast of New Zealand. There is pain and anguish, and we are responsible for turning the cries and screams of birds and beasts back into chirps, barks, and growls; we bear the burden of transforming the cacophony of pain into a chorus of lively, noisy creatures.

In the gravity of our plight and in the depth of our despair, as our ship of state splinters into pieces, spinning around and around, coming closer, and making us sick from its gyre, the wonders of the world slowly disappear from view. We need hope, yes, but we need so much more. As the cliché goes, we need to find our own moral compass, our own ethical gyroscope; we need a critical Manifesto to guide us, a leader to inspire us, a plan to get this weary Earth replanted and restored, re-imagined for a life re-aligned.

We all stand in need of immediate, direct action that will bring the planet back to its health. If we can then learn the lesson of forbearance, of leaving all living things alone, and stop managing the forests and shooting the critters, both large and small, damming the rivers and streams and killing the fish, we might then know that rejuvenating feeling called *vibrancy.* We must remember the imperative: Stop the burning of fossil fuels.

Exhilaration might take us one step further into restoration. First, we must find some way to climb out of our own despair, to rid ourselves of the excuse of not knowing what to do and when to do it, for ignorance produces more destruction. We must take action that will turn aside the entrepreneurial rage that has been released over so many decades against all that is magnificent, essential, wondrous and, when we allow ourselves to admit it, that is miraculous.

The entomologist A. O. Wilson makes the following, shocking claim: "If all mankind were to disappear, the world would regenerate back to the rich state of equilibrium that existed ten thousand years ago. If insects were to vanish, the environment would collapse into chaos." His claim is not about which is more important, a pest or a person. It is an insight about dependence and interdependence, and one that realigns our alleged importance in the vast scheme of nature.

Our acts of reawakened care and kindness must be inscribed deep within us, and deep within our only home, our *oikos.* Ecology is not a term. It is an address, the place of our dwelling. We must do all we can to make people take note of the wonder of the world, and we must do it in this instant. How to do that is difficult, near impossible, but it is imperative. It must happen in prose and in poetry, in song, painting, petitions, in political action, and raucous demonstrations. It must happen in praying, seeing, and listening, in reading and in lecturing, knowing that everything, everywhere, now survives under threat of extinction. We must issue our own living Manifesto.

Herman Melville allowed himself to get so entangled in prose, and to wander so widely in the bible because he found everyday language inert, lacking the power to arouse sleepers into wakefulness, so they would know those mighty themes he believed so crucial to the salvation of the natural world. The bible was a sourcebook for starting over, an incipit and an alarm for uncovering the wonder of nature: There, in Genesis, Moby Dick swims for the very first time. There, in Homer and Shakespeare, people shout the truth to the gods, as if for the very first time. Melville needed us to start over and to begin anew. He relied on Homer, a poet of passages, who might have been commenting on us: "Odysseus awoke out of his sleep in his native land. Yet he knew it not after his long absence."

Herman Melville, as an author, failed to sell books and disappointed the critics. But if Melville did fail, if he did appear odd, it was because readers and critics failed him. There is no wondering here: He did not make reading or understanding easy. And thus, he was misunderstood or understood not at all. People had the correct reaction. Melville intended *Moby Dick* to be supremely difficult, for it was a signal and a warning to those who, much later, might ponder the meaning of millions of whales hunted to death, and a shocking 140 species of cetaceans now extinct.

And thus, *Moby Dick* comes to us not as a crippled or convoluted novel, but as a Manifesto of the most outsized, oversized proportions, meant to be read with foresight. It has no future tense for good reason—only we can give it a future. *Moby Dick* comes to us possessed, equally, of the deepest belief, infused with the most essential and most fundamental of all rescues—not solely of humankind, but of animals, plants, trees, grasses—of all that grows and struggles to survive.

Moby Dick thus cannot be compared with any other work of prose; and it certainly will not stand up, in the middle of the nineteenth century, against anything from that usually lulling, satisfying genre, fiction. The book is not that, and Melville most certainly has no intent to give us something easy and pleasing: He aims to unsettle readers rather than to resettle them. A sea adventure and a land tragedy, *Moby Dick* encompasses the environment because it is so deeply concerned with the survival of all sentient life. Melville went after the incipient greed that exploded in the middle of the nineteenth century, its pools of blood floating on the waves, a preamble to the oil that came gushing from the ground, poisoning everything, bringing nature to its knees, killing off a good deal of the natural world and arriving at a tragic close in the early decades of the twenty-first century.

Melville takes us on an oceanic voyage by rekindling the very beginnings of literature in the West, with *The Iliad*; with its very first emotion, rage; with a reworking of the bible for his own purposes; and finally, with a recalibrating of the arc of our understanding about commerce and its inherent brutality, as the two—capitalism and creation—came crashing together in the middle of the nineteenth century. Melville, who in his youth took up a weapon against whales, intent on killing, dropped his sword in the sea, jumped ship, and scrambled home to sound an alarm.

He looked at killing on the high seas and was repulsed by his own arrogance. He confronted his own maniacal captain, and was appalled. He knew the destruction of nature firsthand and he fled from his own behavior. But he fled with enough time, and enough care, to pick up a new weapon, one that revealed his own heart and thus left us with his lasting will and testament. His father-in-law, as Chief-Justice, insulated that national pandemic called greed from attack through his passing of myriad laws. Deep into pleasure and eager for distraction, people needed to learn how to read Melville's tale of injustice. That took time. Now, we have run out of time. But it has slowly happened: We now see. Now, we must do.

And so, that master of the ultimatum, Herman Melville, as if he were eyewitness to the Incipit of Creation, itself, reached far back in time for essentials. Herman Melville is the magus of the nineteenth century and thus knows how to align the power of language with the immensity of the Earth. An Ishmael of his own making, he speaks the truth about the collusion of Creation/Destruction, of killing at a most foundational level, at the level of the leviathans. And thus, the man with a quill makes demands: Read and learn. Read and believe. Read and take action. Read and undertake an amazing excursion into wonder and then take action. Every savior must try to save.

But, above all and beyond everything else, Melville wants us to know that any attempt on the life of Moby Dick means the destruction of the heart and soul of creation, the erasure of the sacred. We must remember that Ahab has been driven out of his mind, shouting his orders and cursing his world, all the while with only one leg to stand on, off balance in all senses: What he succeeds in destroying most effectively and most thoroughly, in the end, is his own humanity. His rage, so degraded from that of its ancient order, no longer ennobles. First a leg, then his balance, and a bit later his reason, a captain without a *capet*, an awful state of being beyond madness. Moby Dick escapes, destroying the Pequod and its crew, depriving investors of profit. In a capitalist society, that is reason for deep mourning.

We must put a stop to those who continue to hold in their hands a lethal weapon, eager to kill, ready to profit from emptying the Earth of its resources, digging deep into its heart for treasure, wrenching shiny objects out of the streams and oceans—mining every speck and sparkle of what has come to be called the biosphere. We must meet those villains head on and prevent them from continuing to dismantle the natural world—as if no one noticed, as if they had replaced their silly divots in this cosmic game, making things appear alright once again, until all of the green world that so comforts and keeps us sane—the last fleck of every feather, leaf, and scale—has finally disappeared, and we find ourselves trying to live in a relic of the once-resplendent world. Science run amok has replaced grass with astroturf, edited the genetic constitutions of salmon and apples, as if they were works of fiction, through something called CRISPR technology, cloned mice and rabbits, reduced people to robots, and thinking to a chat with some bot. The result, to repeat, is nature de-natured, life de-vivified, the whole of the natural world, its four elements poisoned with "forever chemicals," 4,700 of them, none of which occurs naturally, all of which get concocted in laboratories and set loose on the baffled as well as the true believers.

In 1851, in what many critics had come to agree was his overstuffed and derivative tall tale—the Big One that got away—Herman Melville pulled off something radically different. He paid homage to the first creatures in creation, so utterly majestic and powerfully defiant, they stood in for the definition of wonder. *Moby Dick* presents mammals as critical lessons: We must refuse to be destroyed by those who, through rage and greed, dismantle our habitat, and who, at the very same time, try to convince us that they are taking us into a future that will shine brighter and longer, promising us diamonds and handing out rhinestones. The reign of the snake-oil salesman continues.

We must embrace the natural world as it is—on life support, gasping, threatening to flat-line and disappear for good. Such horror carries with it obvious implications: Imagination, which now seems to be the sole possession of science/technology, can only design solutions with ever-more serious side effects. Some master-minds of technology tell us we should relax, forget it all, and imagine another, more invigorating life that beckons anew on Mars. We must change our minds, our own nature, and then attend to nature at large— all of it on this planet, on the *Earth,* the only planet in the solar system whose name does not derive from Greco/Roman mythology, and whose etymological root, from the Anglo-Saxon, means "ground" or "soil." (We must, of course, account for those mighty oceans.) The word *earth* first appears in England's earliest epic, in *Beowulf,* in a key moment in the poem, when the warrior Hygelac gives up fighting by laying his sword to rest in the earth.

Melville, himself, delights in playing with etymological roots, especially the Hebrew *livyatan,* meaning "twisting" "turning," "winding," or "coiling." Moby

Dick dominates as the Laocooan of the open ocean. For Melville, this is Adamic naming. At the end of *Moby Dick*, we readers, who have survived it all, are left with an image, or afterimage, embodied in the might of Moby Dick. For the whale has forced onto the book a decisive conclusion that emboldens and enlightens: One of the largest animals on Earth has escaped with its life, with the Pequod's ropes still wound around its massive body, its ability to twist and coil contorted into a gyrating death.

And so, we must shift our focus away from Ahab, Gabriel, or even Ishmael and, at the close of the narration, pay attention to the heroic survivor of the tale, who will have to be named in order to become a character anew, but whose name does not reveal its essence. From a creature hunted as a repository of resources, Moby Dick has become a model for the most crucial of lessons. A fish with fins for almost the entirety of the narrative, the bull whale ends as mammal and major character. The title of the book, *Moby Dick; or, the Whale*, encapsulates its theme, for Moby Dick, so named, belongs to Ahab for most of the story, and manages to reclaim its own nature, at the end of the telling, as the Whale or, more accurately, as the leviathan.

As creatures of the mighty twist and miraculous turn, whales emerge out of the Ur-spin, the centrifugal force that shapes creation. The whale thus mimics a universe that, wound-up but exhausted, continues to whirl as a gigantic centrifuge, its motion reflected in the word, *universe*, from Latin *verso,* "to turn," and thus the world enduring as a *uni-versal,* or "one-ness" of centrifugal power. And, out of that universal turning emerges the harmony, the ancient symphony of the spheres. The vortex down below, into which the Pequod gets sucked, revolves in an opposite direction, a centripetal pull, sucking all things into its center, deep into its center, spiraling them down and farther down to their demise. It is that primal, powerful force that Ishmael miraculously survives.

As first in line, Moby Dick entered the world with the deepest meaning of its aboriginal turning. Like a spiral, the whale is both beginning and ending, a turn in a universe that revolves at 1,000 miles per hour, completing its circuit every twenty-four hours. To destroy the leviathan, in a sacred sense, is to attack creation at its heart, at the revolve of the universe. To kill the whale forces the circling of the spheres into an eccentric and finally into chaos. Moby Dick mocks the Pequod's death spiral.

Whales are the first, the largest, the most puzzling, and one of the most miraculous of all creatures, swimming with few of us ever catching sight of their majesty, singing with very few of us ever hearing their songs. It is a creature, of course, that delights as spectacle, ordinary but miraculous. Moby Dick carries an additional layer of the unbelievable, for it is not merely a bull Sperm whale but one beyond brown and beyond white, a rarity among all creatures. Melville offers us that oddity, not so much as symbol, but as mimetic example. The white whale as albino is persistently present, so pure as to turn invisible, so radiant as to blind, with a light that shines as if from a deity.

Moby Dick escapes to the infinitude that is the sea and to the safety that is its home, surviving the rage of a madman and the onslaught of harpooners, but its freedom, hard-won and bloody, is less than a triumph. For that magnificent creature has been wounded, perhaps at levels we cannot know, perhaps mortally. No matter, for Moby Dick has escaped and, for the moment, swims free in its habitat. Such a victory, albeit a slightly degraded one, suggests that there might be hope for us, a chance to heed the warnings and to allow the rest of nature to continue living within its own freedom and, not just to save the Earth, but to grab hold of our own beleaguered selves, as well.

In order to take decisive action, we must change our own minds—hang up our harpoons, throw down our swords forever—and save this most spectacular earth we call home, one that we share with myriad inhabitants. Melville has given us a most powerful, necessary warning, alerting us to the horrific violence that people are capable of inflicting on nature. We must take heed; we must pay attention. What should that primal act of our own salvation look like? The entomologist, A.O. Wilson, once again, offers some apposite wisdom: "The only hope for the species still living is a human effort commensurate with the magnitude of the problem."

Melville has handed us a charge, in the form of a most powerful Manifesto, one that directs and requires us to make "a human effort commensurate with the magnitude of the problem." At this moment, the prognosis for the environment could not be grimmer, the predictions not more dire, for far too many climate scientists predict the loss of, well, everything, and in a very short order—at most, three decades. And so, in a state of ecological despair, arriving at the end of our reading of *Moby Dick; or, The Whale,* we might all feel tempted to say, and perhaps to no one in particular, but rather to the universe: Alright, go ahead, call me Ishmael, because, like our narrator, we, too, feel orphaned and stranded; we have drifted out of our element, lone survivors in desperate need of a miraculous rescue.

It is a state that Melville seems to favor. In an essay titled "Hawthorne and His Mosses," which he published six-months into the writing of *Moby Dick*, in August 1850, Melville suggested that all important books should be treated as orphans, as if written *ex nihilo*: "Would that all excellent books were foundlings, without father or mother, that so it might be, we could glorify them, without including their ostensible authors." (Here is Melville saying, Call me nothing; take my identity, for I, too, am an orphan, just another side of Ishamael.) By extension, people might need to be conceived as creations alive without parents, miracles akin to the whale, or what the ancients called *venire ad vitam sine genitore*: "To come to life without begetting," or, in more miraculous ways, akin to Athena, the Godddess of Wisdom, who was born fully formed from the forehead of her father, Zeus.

Unlike Ishmael, we cannot rely on some life-saving Rachel to pluck us out of the water, even though history is rich with rescues of deserving cast-offs and likeable orphans: Moses and Superman come to mind. It is a yearning, this desire to be rescued by some outside force, the highest order of wish fulfillment. But it will not happen. The great many of us may not have caused such fundamental destruction, but we all must now devote our lives to this environmental catastrophe, and pry lose the grip that corporate America has on nature's throat, and allow the Earth to return to a state that approaches normal—if such a thing is even possible any longer. All this must be an effort, not of the coercive *we* of the Declaration of Independence, but of the enthusiastic *us* of the Melville Manifesto.

The atmosphere can tolerate no more poisoning— none. In order to limit global warming to 1.5 degrees Celsius above pre-industrial levels, the limit set by the Paris Agreements, global carbon-dioxide emissions must be reduced to Net Zero by 2050. To take that indomitable project called Progress in a reverse direction, to eradicate the goals of development and advancement, will require the most radical arguments and solutions, but what greater crisis could we possibly confront than the end of the Earth? In spite of what some technophiles believe they can pull off, animal extinction is not reversible.

We must undertake, immediately, the most outlandish, outrageous, totally unbelievable and unrealistic project for the recovery of the Earth: We must stop killing everything that takes a breath or moves. At this very moment, we must collaborate, corroborate, and undertake nothing less than the resuscitation of our own sanity. Far too many experts conclude that we have several decades, and certainly no more than three, before we must face facts, surrender hope, and watch our ship of state, our own water-logged and pock-marked Pequod, get sucked into the centrifuge and sink out of view.

BARRY SANDERS is the Founding Co-chair at the Oregon Institute for Creative Research-E4. He has twice been a finalist for the Pulitzer Prize and is the author of fourteen books and over fifty essays and articles, including *Sudden Glory*, *Alienable Rights* (winner of the Robert F. Kennedy Human Rights Award; with Francis Adams), *ABC* (with Ivan Illich), *The Private Death of Public Discourse*, and *A Is for Ox*.

Printed and bound by CPI Group (UK) Ltd, Croydon, CR0 4YY

22/04/2025

01849892-0002